leave you with either a smile on your face or a tear in your eye. And I challenge you to finish the entire book without breaking into a full-on sob!"

—KELLIE RASBERRY EVANS, co-host of the *Kidd Kraddick Morning Show* and co-host of *A Sandwich and Some Lovin'* podcast

"Stoney Stamper takes you on his journey from old-fashioned cowboy to modern family man in this heartfelt look at fatherhood, love, and life off the beaten path."

—ALLY CARTER, *New York Times* best-selling author

"For any movie or television show you've ever loved, you probably loved it because the creators made you feel a personal connection to the characters. Stoney Stamper tapped into the same vein for this book. You will love it because he makes it personal and lets you into his family. You'll want to come back and visit."

—JIMMIE TRAMEL, author and *Tulsa World* pop-culture writer

"Fun, honest, and necessary. There aren't many options for fathers and men out there sharing truth and keeping it real. Stoney manages to offer that in an engaging and hilarious way. We may have the new Rick Bragg with decidedly less grump."

—KALAN CHAPMAN LLOYD, award-winning author and attorney

"Stoney has a way with words like no other. Having four kids myself, two of whom are daughters, I found myself relating to many of his stories and at times actually pulling for him, as I have lived some of these same events. Through changing diapers, changing hormones, and everything that comes with being a father to beautiful daughters, I am a fan. Stoney is to words as Robert Earl Keen is to music."

—Josh West, majority leader for the Oklahoma House of Representatives

"As a happily married father of three who often feels light years away from the life I imagined and the one I have (in the best imaginable way), I've found a companion in Stoney Stamper and his bittersweet book *My First Rodeo*. Stoney took me on a reflective journey filled with tangibly relatable anecdotes and markedly honest commentary —one where I found myself fully immersed in a parallel cathartic experience. Stoney's honest tone, subtle humor, and ability to capture the fragility of time and the power of love made this a refreshing and memorable read."

—Daniel Patterson, author of *The Assertive Parent*

"*My First Rodeo* is a captivating story of one man's adventure in all things family. The author takes his audience by the hand, one page at a time, and reminds us that what we think we don't want just might be the best thing that could ever happen to us. Few authors . . . few men, even, are so transparent and honest with the struggles, elations, fears, joys, and even challenges that encompass the journey of parenthood. Funny and emotional, *My First Rodeo* is a must-read. A story of love, maybe even of destiny, Stamper's endearing tale will leave you wanting more and will evoke a deep need to find your own way back home."

—Veronica Hix, executive director of ONABEN

"This book builds the bridge between feeling normal and parenthood. Hilarious and relatable, Stoney captivates your attention as he walks you through the beauty and hardships of being the father of a blended family."

—Catrina Hermenet, blogger and creator
of @mommystruth

Foreword by CATHERINE FREDERICK, *Do South Magazine*

My First RODEO

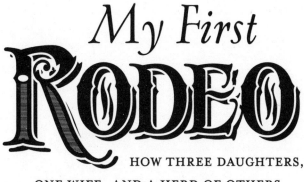

HOW THREE DAUGHTERS, ONE WIFE, AND A HERD OF OTHERS ARE MAKING ME A BETTER DAD

STONEY STAMPER

of The Daddy Diaries blog

WATERBROOK

MY FIRST RODEO

All Scripture quotations are taken from the Holy Bible, New International Version®, NIV®. Copyright © 1973, 1978, 1984 by Biblica Inc.® Used by permission. All rights reserved worldwide.

Hardcover ISBN 978-0-7352-9165-2
eBook ISBN 978-0-7352-9166-9

Copyright © 2019 by Stoney Stamper

Cover design by Kristopher K. Orr; barn cover photo by Frank Staub, Getty Images; author cover photo and interior photos by April Stamper, 13:13 Photography

Published in the United States by WaterBrook, an imprint of the Crown Publishing Group, a division of Penguin Random House LLC, New York.

WATERBROOK® and its deer colophon are registered trademarks of Penguin Random House LLC.

Names: Stamper, Stoney, author.
Title: My first rodeo : how three daughters, one wife, and a herd of others are making me a better dad / Stoney Stamper.
Description: First Edition. | Colorado Springs : WaterBrook, 2019.
Identifiers: LCCN 2018041312| ISBN 9780735291652 (hardcover) | ISBN 9780735291669 (electronic)
Subjects: LCSH: Fatherhood—Religious aspects—Christianity. | Fathers—Religious life. | Christian men—United States.
Classification: LCC BV4529.17 .S73 2019 | DDC 248.8/421—dc23
LC record available at https://lccn.loc.gov/2018041312

Printed in the United States of America
2019—First Edition

10 9 8 7 6 5 4 3 2 1

SPECIAL SALES
Most WaterBrook books are available at special quantity discounts when purchased in bulk by corporations, organizations, and special-interest groups. Custom imprinting or excerpting can also be done to fit special needs. For information, please email special marketscms@penguinrandomhouse.com or call 1-800-603-7051.

To April, not a single word of this book would have been possible without you. My real life started the day our paths crossed again. You are the June to my Johnny, and I love you more than you can know.

To my daughters—Abby, Emma, and Gracee— thank you for giving me the only job that has ever really mattered in my life. Being a dad. Pineapple.

Contents

Contents

Foreword

It was 2013 and I was scrolling through social media when I came upon an image of this beautiful Australian shepherd, which pulled me in. Then I started reading the words beneath the photo. Beautiful words. Funny words. Raw words. It was a heartfelt telling of a man losing his best furry friend, written by a man I didn't know: Stoney Stamper. I finished reading. I dried my eyes. I kept scrolling.

The next day, I probably shared his story with at least ten people. I couldn't stop thinking about it. That's the thing about good storytelling; it leaps off the page and into your mind and makes its home there. I started digging. I had to figure out who this Stoney Stamper guy was. It didn't take long to find him and his regular musings at his blog, *The Daddy Diaries*. I read every post. I laughed. Hard. I cried. Big tears. I knew I had to reach out and get this guy to write for my magazine, *Do South*. I had built the magazine on great storytelling and had a group of stellar writers. What I didn't have was someone writing with so much humor.

I contacted Stoney, and our friendship was born. Each month he'd let my readers into the life of his family. I got a front-row seat as his children grew older and as his wife's photography business blossomed. I was lucky.

And now you are too.

You may be drawn to this book because you have a blended family. There's nothing quite like marrying someone with children. In an instant you take on new responsibilities and do your best to be an instant parent.

If this has happened to you, you know it can be like running an obstacle course blindfolded. It can also stretch you in ways you didn't know were possible. Your heart opens. You find yourself suddenly singing kids' songs in the shower. You learn to love mac and cheese, and chicken nuggets. And all of a sudden you realize that while you're not the coolest kid on the block anymore, you are so happy!

Even if your background is different from Stoney's, you'll love going along for the ride as he finds his footing as a husband and father. Stoney's stories are epically funny, but they're also tender reflections on love and parenting.

I still remember the joy I felt when I discovered Stoney's writing and asked him to be a part of *Do South Magazine*. I'm good at scouting out talent, and I knew his words would resonate with my audience. It may be because his stories feel timeless and a bit untamed. Like a cowboy. One who has finally found the perfect place to hang his hat.

—Catherine Frederick,
owner and editor-in-chief of *Do South Magazine*

Introduction

ONE SUNNY DAY MORE THAN five years ago, I sat down with my then six-week-old daughter, Gracee June. I was a man in my midthirties who had sworn time and again that I'd never be a father. I'd tell anyone who would listen. While nearly all my similarly aged friends and family had already started families, and several of them had children in their teens, I was only just beginning mine. Gracee was my first, and only, biological child. A few years prior to this sunny day, I had married my childhood sweetheart, and she had two daughters, Abby and Emma. Those two little girls had spent the last two years giving me daily lessons on how to be a father, and I was learning, albeit slowly. A baptism by fire, of sorts. I had no idea what I was doing, but I tried hard. Gracee—she was my first baby. I was thirty-three years old and had never changed a diaper. Never given a baby a bath. Never fed or burped a tiny little body over my shoulder.

On that fateful day, my wife, April, had decided to use her Mother's Day gift from me and the girls: a spa day complete with a deep-tissue massage, facial, manicure, and pedicure. A day of relaxation that she certainly deserved. When she left that day, we had no idea it would put into motion something beyond our wildest dreams. It was the first time I had ever spent the day alone with our precious little girl. I was blindly confident that the day would go smoothly. I am a competent person, after all. This couldn't be that hard, right? As it would turn out, it was harder than expected. And everything that *could* go wrong *did* go wrong. And just like Abby and Emma had done, Gracee, in a mere matter of moments, shattered any illusions that I knew what I was doing. But I'm an optimist, and I believed something good was going to come from that day, shattered illusions and all.

That evening I decided to take my sense of humor and knack for storytelling to pen and paper. I told the story of all of the craziness that had occurred that first day alone as daddy and daughter. I posted our story that night to my personal Facebook page, sort of hoping to get a few laughs. The story was shared over one thousand times in the first day. Our funny little story brought more laughs than anticipated, and it continued to make the rounds on social media for a few more weeks. Now, I had been a writer, in my own mind, for most of my life. I kept journals and wrote poems and short stories. But nothing anyone had ever really read, besides myself. April began encouraging me to start a Facebook page for my writing, maybe even a parenting blog. I confess that writing was a good release for me. I enjoyed it. And it was free, wouldn't cost us anything except maybe a little bit of ego, if it didn't take off.

I told April that I would try it but only continue to do it if I could get at least one thousand followers. I thought this was a lofty goal. Well, much to my surprise, I had more than one thousand followers in the first day. Next thing I knew, I had five thousand. And then ten thousand. We had officially gone viral. Today my blog—

The Daddy Diaries—reaches more than one hundred thousand people every day. April and I still sit around sort of shocked. Who could have ever seen that coming?! Well, not us, that's for sure. *The Daddy Diaries* has evolved into its own community, even being a place where people come to help others. In the last five years, we have raised more than sixty thousand dollars for families and children in need. We have been fortunate enough to help more than fifty families in times of trouble or tragedy. Again, we never saw that coming.

We've tried to take this opportunity and use it to make the world a little better place. But we've also been able to use it to show our daughters what a joy it is to help others, to show kindness and love to people that haven't been as fortunate as we have. Actually, *fortunate* is not the best word choice. The better word is *blessed*. If you had told me ten years ago I would be the dad to three generous-hearted daughters, husband to my very best friend (April Skinner, more about her later), and the author of a popular parenting blog, I would've laughed in your face after I'd picked myself up off the ground from laughing so hard. And I expect that most anyone who knew me would have fallen down laughing right alongside me. But for some reason, God decided to do one of those "old chunk of coal but gonna be a diamond someday" routines. He took the reins of my life and steered me right where I was supposed to be. Yep, God dropped me right in the middle of a whirlpool full of estrogen and laughter and a few tears, because girls cry a little. And just as he did on the day he finished making the heavens and the earth, he looked at me knee deep in it and said, "Now, that's good."

And as usual, God was right. It's so good.

I was born on June 29, 1979. I was born into a quarter-horse ranching family. Back in those days you had to stay in the hospital for at least three days before you could take your baby home, so I was exactly three days old the first time I sat on a horse. It was my granddad's tradition. Bring the babies home and then put them on a horse—with him holding us, of course. This went for me and all my siblings and cousins. Stampers were meant to be on horseback, he believed, so you started them young. As young as possible. We all had our own horses as soon as we were physically able to ride by ourselves. Many of these horses had been passed down from generation to generation. We had a couple of Shetlands for the smaller kids, and these were actually the same ponies my own dad had ridden as a kid, before graduating to a full-sized horse. Their names were Surprise and Teeny Tonette. Surprise was Teeny Tonette's mother. By the time I came along, Surprise was thirty-six years old, and Tonette was thirty-two, which is extremely elderly in equine years.

If you aren't familiar with horses, Shetlands have a bit of a reputation for being ornery and sometimes having flat-out mean dispositions. But they were little, and they were broke to death, so anyone could crawl all over them and they'd take good care of us. That doesn't mean they wouldn't take a small bite out of you if they saw the opportunity. But according to my granddad and dad, that was just part of growing up a rancher. I was the oldest grandson. So I was expected to be tough. My grandpa would tell me that the ranch would be mine someday and that I had to learn all I could about horses and cows. Learn to train, learn to have a good eye for horseflesh. Know when someone is trying to swindle you. Horse traders don't have a great reputation for a reason. They are well known for doctoring up a lame horse and trying to sell him for a retail price. I was taught to look beyond that and see the horse, see the details most people don't see. And I was pretty dang good at it.

We had bucking chutes on one end of the arena and had bull buck-outs often at the ranch. Hundreds of people would pile into our indoor arenas on Friday and Saturday nights to watch people riding bulls. We'd buck out fifty on a Friday night and fifty-one on a Saturday night. It was called the Stamper Ranch 101 Bull Buck-Out, and it was fun. We had them for years until one of the promoters that helped put the event on wanted to start selling alcohol in the concession stands. My grandfather, the son of an evangelist and a very devout member of the Murphy Church of God, was having none of it. No way. Not a chance. He was a man of principle. He didn't care if it meant losing money. He wasn't going to do it. He'd say a prayer before each of the bucking events, asking for the safety of those participating and for everyone who came to have a safe trip home. It was a great childhood, I'm not going to lie. We also had a kids' event at each performance.

When I was five years old, I was entered into the calf-riding event. I straddled the little black calf; my dad tightened my rope around my hand and told me, "Squeeze tight with your legs, buddy. Keep your right hand up, stay in the middle of him, and you'll do fine." I slid up close to my rope like I'd been taught, squeezed with my legs, and nodded my head for the gate to be opened. The little calf jumped out of the chute and began to buck down the pen. I did everything my dad told me to. And I rode him! As I fell off after the buzzer, the little hundred-pound calf stepped on my head, scuffing up my forehead a little bit, but more importantly, he stomped a hole in my black Resistol cowboy hat. I was not a happy boy. I wasn't as concerned with my bleeding head as I was with the hole in my precious hat. I picked it up and dusted it off and stared in horror at my hat. My uncle Larry came running out to me and gave me a high five. "Good ride, Stone!" I won the money that night. A whopping twenty-dollar bill. My uncle, being funny, folded it up and stuck it in the hole in the brim of my hat. My dad ran up to me with a big smile and said, "You did great! Exactly what I said. Good job, buddy."

That was my first rodeo. My first *actual* rodeo. I went on to show cutting horses, which is what my family actually did for a living. As a teenager, and on into college, I broke young horses to ride that we raised, and rode some outside horses for other people who didn't want to risk getting bucked off. I liked it. I made enough money in college to keep my head above water, and I always enjoyed it. Now that I am getting a little older and I've had back surgeries and hip surgeries and knee surgeries, getting on a young bucking colt isn't exactly ideal. I miss it, and I'd love to do it, but I'm pretty sure my wife would kill me if she saw me crawling on the back of a waspy, snorting two-year-old. But nothing beats the feeling of taking that wild animal and becoming one with it. Teaching it manners and giving it a purpose. Making a good horse for someone to rope calves on, or taking it to do hard ranch work. Nothing beats that feeling.

However, in 2011, when I met the trio of girls from Ketchum, Oklahoma, I was embarking on a journey that was most decidedly something out of my comfort zone. It was new. It was scary. I had no idea what to say and do with little girls. This ol' cowboy may get throwed, as the saying goes, but I was still gonna saddle up and give it a try. And my goodness, what a ride it has been. Trust me, I've been "throwed" more times than I can count. But just as I was taught once when I was four years old, riding Teeny Tonette in our arena and something spooked her, causing her to jump out from under me, a real cowboy dusts himself off and climbs right back on. Sometimes that is hard to do. Fear, pain, pride—all of that has to be put aside. You grit your teeth and you mount back up and try to learn from what you did wrong the last time. Some problems are harder than others. Some are more difficult to overcome. I've had seven years of fatherhood now, and I still get "throwed" from time to time, but certainly less often than I did in the beginning. And just like breaking in new colts, sometimes just when you think that you've got a good seat, and that the colt's had all the rough ridden off of him, he decides to break in two, blowing and snorting and bucking. And you may find yourself lying in the dust, wondering what in the world just happened. It may hurt a little. But you can't give up on him, just like you wouldn't give up on your kids. You walk back over to him, or limp over to him in my case. You calm him down and remind him that you're there to help. And then you climb right back into the saddle for another run.

Kids aren't so much different. They start feeling comfortable; then something happens. Who knows what it is? But I have learned there is only one way to approach them. And that is with patience. You can't rush it or they'll get spooked and run away. Show them you're not going to hurt them, that you're only doing what's best for them, and eventually they'll realize you are their partner and not their enemy. Turns out, rodeos and raising kids aren't so much different after all.

That's what the rest of this book is about—learning to be a dad. But also about learning to be a husband, and a brother, and a son, and a man.

The Story of Us

INCE I AM A ROOKIE AUTHOR here in the realm of book writing, or a greenhorn, in cowboy terms, I have tinkered around with several different ways to begin the book. Maybe a funny story? Perhaps a touching story of the first time I finally bonded with Abby, my then-new eleven-year-old stepdaughter? Or possibly the time I sent Emma to school wearing only pantyhose? Trust me, I've got a lot of options. But I guess before I can tell you about any of that, I have to tell you how we got here in the first place. So I suppose the best place to start is at the beginning (duh). I'm asked this question quite often: "How did the story of you and April begin?" And that's a pretty good story actually, so that's how I'll get things started.

Even though we have only been together now for seven years, our story started long before that. I grew up in a little place called Murphy, Oklahoma. It's between Locust Grove and Chouteau, off of Highway 412. Growing up, I lived in two different houses, and they were only about four hundred yards from each other. No matter how long I've been gone, when I think of home, I think of Murphy.

When I was ten years old, this little girl and her family moved in just down the road a ways. She was just over a year younger than me. A little brunette with a few freckles. And she was spunky—coincidentally, a lot like my daughter Emma. This little girl's name was April Skinner. We rode bus number five to school together, then back home, every day. She started going to church at Murphy Church of God, where my family and I went and where my grandpa was the preacher. So we saw each other almost every day. We became friends.

But here's the deal. She had a *wicked* mad crush on me, and she wasn't subtle about it. She flirted with me constantly. We have a close mutual friend who was always the mediator, and even into our teen-age years they were always plotting. They think I didn't know what was going on, but I did. When we went on trips with the church, it was always the three of us together, with April in the middle. One time we went to Eureka Springs, Arkansas, to watch the passion play, and it was freezing. "Hey, Stoney, we've got a blanket we could cover up with. But we'll need to cuddle, you know, for the warmth." Wow, how convenient. And as usual, April was in the middle.

I remember another example from the time our church had a lock-in for the youth group. Now, a lock-in is basically just a big sleepover in the church building, and you play games and watch movies and stuff all night long. I was fourteen, almost fifteen, and

April was thirteen. After several hours of activities at the lock-in, most of the kids started winding down around three or four in the morning. The sleeping bags, blankets, pillows, and such were spread out on the floor to make pallets for us all to lie on. April and I ended up "near" each other. Wow, how convenient. Actually, very near. Too near. Near enough that we probably should've been reprimanded because of the nearness that we shared in the house of the Lord. And we almost kissed. *Almost.* We were having a moment, and the fourteen-year-old me choked. I just couldn't do it. I don't know why. Maybe it was because I thought Jesus was watching. Or maybe it was because we were in a church. Of course, it may have been that I was just chicken. Yeah, that's probably it. Anyway, we didn't kiss, and April turned fourteen not long after. And then she moved away.

I don't think I saw April again until our crafty old friend Jennifer got married. April was a bridesmaid, and I was an usher. April wasn't fourteen any longer. She looked more grown up, and very pretty. Except she had this weird, short haircut, and it was maroon. But hey, it was the nineties. We all had some funky haircuts back then, so no big deal. But get this. At the wedding, I could hardly even get her to pay attention to me. I tried smiling, saying hello. Yes, she was undoubtedly doing her best to ignore me. She'll even admit to it now, she was trying to be cool. So I saw April for a bit, sort of, and then not again for another twelve long years.

Then one day I got a friend request on Facebook. It was from a lady named April Johnston. Her profile picture looked fairly familiar, but different. Yet I swear I knew those eyes and smile. I messaged her and asked, "Is this April Skinner?" To which she emphatically replied, "YES!" We chatted briefly, and then a few months went by with no contact. One afternoon I was enjoying a much-needed break on a patio in Fort Worth, Texas, and posted a picture on Facebook of me giving a thumbs-up. She saw it, thought I looked cute (I guess), and liked the picture. And then she proceeded to like every other picture I had on Facebook. My phone pretty much exploded and melted down from all the notifications. Now, from a guy's perspective, you've got to weigh your options here. From looking at her pictures, I knew she was a very attractive woman. But after she liked all my photos, I got a little worried she might have a bit of the *Single White Female* in her. Or maybe even the lady in *Fatal Attraction* who boiled the bunny rabbit. Yeah, scary. But thankfully, there were no rabbits or single white men harmed in this story, and April turned out to be the most awesome woman I've ever known.

It's been almost thirty years now since we first met. I could've never imagined back then the impact she would someday have on my life. That we'd someday be married and have three beautiful daughters. That we'd live in a beautiful spot in Texas. I couldn't have guessed any of that. But I guess that's the cool part about life. It has a tendency to work itself out if you'll just have a little faith and let it. I spent at least a dozen years chasing this elusive happiness. I looked for it in my job. I looked for it in relationships that were completely wrong for me. I moved to Florida for a few years. I moved to Virginia for a few more after that. I drove a Mercedes and wore a Rolex because that's what everyone around me drove and wore. I gradually became someone I didn't really like, someone who was so far from whom he was raised to be. I felt completely lost. But then one day, as if it were a prayer I didn't know I was praying, the happiness I'd been chasing landed right in my lap. It wasn't in Florida, lying on the beach. It wasn't in Virginia, driving fancy cars or wearing expensive watches. It was living on a little farm in East Texas, with one wife, three daughters, and tons of animals. And absolutely having the time of my life, with the very best friend I have ever had.

Over the Hill

MY BACK HURTS. ACTUALLY, MY BACK has hurt for about three years now. Honestly, I have had back problems for about eighteen years, following a pretty bad accident I had in 2000. An eleven-thousand-pound horse trailer fell on top of me, literally. It's a long story for another day, but it definitely left its mark on my body.

Usually after visiting a chiropractor and getting a cortisone shot or two, I can get things back to normal, or at least what I consider normal. But this one day in November, on Thanksgiving Day of all days, I woke up with a backache. Nothing out of the ordinary, so I limped around my mother-in-law's house all day, took some Advil, and moved around as slowly as possible. A week later I went to the chiropractor and got twisted and popped and cracked, but I was still having a really hard time. The steroid shots that generally got me over the hump did absolutely nothing. The pain in my back and the pain shooting down my right leg were different than they had been in the past and were excruciating. The doctor decided I should get some X-rays and an MRI, so I did. After the MRI, they said they'd call me in the following week with the results. However, before I even got home that day, they called to tell me I had a severely herniated L4-L5 disk. And not only had it herniated, but it had also fragmented, so there was a random piece of my disk floating around loose in my spinal canal. Although it was a relief to find out what was wrong, having back problems of this magnitude is a very scary thing. I mean, I know I am getting older, but I am not exactly ready to hang up my spurs just yet. I am an extremely active person. The best parts of my days aren't spent inside. My favorite things to do are to work outside on our property—building fences, cutting brush, working horses, mowing, weed-eating. Anything outside is where I find my happy place.

So as April and I sat in the surgeon's office listening to him tell me the seriousness of my back issues, a huge dose of reality came crashing down on me like an eleven-thousand-pound horse trailer. He told me, "You'll never be 100 percent again. You've got a lot of damage in there, and we can make you better. However, you are going to have to slow down. You aren't going to be as strong as you once were." Maybe I am a little bit slow, but it wasn't until he said these words to me that I realized exactly what was happening to me. I was getting old.

Getting old! I had always heard my parents and grandparents

talk about it but had never knowingly felt it firsthand. All my life, I have pushed myself to the limit in just about anything I have ever done. I have broken bones. I have had concussions. I have pulled muscles and gotten stitches. I wrestled, played baseball and football, and ran track. As an adult, before I married April and had kids, I lived hard. I spent too much time in saloons, with late nights and little to no sleep. And as they always do, people would tell me I needed to slow down. My parents and siblings worried about me, but I would always laugh and shrug off their advice as nonsense. I knew what my body could handle better than they did, right? One of my coworkers once said about me, "Stoney doesn't burn the candle at both ends. Stoney just throws the whole candle into a bonfire." We all laughed.

But now, as I sit here typing this, I can feel my hip aching. It's a dull ache that stems from that horse trailer accident years ago, and I think to myself, *It's going to rain today. My joints are aching.* Goodness, I am getting old. The life expectancy of an American male is seventy-eight years old, and by that number, I am almost exactly middle aged. My best days are behind me. Now, I know I'm not *that* old. But by the same token, I know I'll never again be quite as strong as I once was. I know I can't work eighteen hours out in the sun, hauling thousands upon thousands of bales of hay, like I once could. And if I get bucked off a horse, I won't bounce back quite as quickly as I used to. Of course, this hurts my cowboy pride. It's hard to admit to myself that I am not the man I was ten years ago.

And then I think back to all the times I was told to "slow down" or to "be careful" or that I was going to "regret that when you're older." And sure, I can see how that may have been wise advice, judging from the scars and aches and pains I have. But I wouldn't change a single thing. I cannot imagine a life where I was more careful. I cannot fathom a younger me slowing down or playing it safe. Going all in, 110 percent, is who I am at my core, and I wouldn't trade that for a million dollars, because I know I have been true to myself and lived my life exactly how I have wanted to, even if it wasn't always smart. Besides, if I didn't do all those stupid things when I was young, then I wouldn't have any funny stories to tell when I am old. And there's nothing I enjoy more than telling funny stories.

So yesterday I watched my crazy little daughter Gracee run 110 miles per hour around the backyard. Now a responsible adult, I hollered, "You need to slow down!" And when she climbed up on top of the patio furniture, I knew there was about a 90 percent chance that she would fall off. So I said to her, "You'd better get down from there. You're going to hurt yourself." And guess what? She ignored me, just like I ignored my parents. Then I grinned and watched as she jumped around like those monkeys on the bed, until the inevitable happened and she fell to the ground. Still grinning, I limped my beaten-up body over to her, dusted her off, and gave her a kiss. Want to make a guess as to what I said? "You've got to be careful. You'll wish you'd listened to me someday." Because apparently that's what you're supposed to say when you get old. Something tells me Gracee's probably not going to realize how true that is. Until she's older, like me. But that's just a hunch.

Safe in His Hands

I T'S A DIFFERENT WORLD TODAY than it was when I was grow-ing up. Yes, that's quite an understatement. I suppose that's true for every generation, if you think about it. Times change, people change, music changes, television changes. And not always for the best, unfortunately. My generation has seen technological advances that generations before me could never have even imagined. But we've also had some unthinkable changes that are scary for a parent to have to deal with these days. During the writing of this book, there have been some unimaginable tragedies carried out right here in our own country, by some of our own citizens. Multiple school shootings, mass shootings at concerts and shopping malls, even churches. It's become dangerous to go to what should be the safest of places. Places where we learn and worship have now turned into places where we have to be watchful and careful of those around us. It's a sad reality, but it is a reality just the same.

One such night, following the horrible school shooting in Parkland, Florida, I sat in my chair with my bad leg elevated and an ice pack on my knee. A few days before, we'd had a toilet start leaking in our master bathroom. It was an old toilet that needed to be replaced anyway. So I went to Lowes that day and bought a new toilet, came home, took the old toilet and wax ring out (which has to be the most disgusting household chore anyone can do), and put the new toilet together and installed it in the bathroom. This was really hard to do for a guy in my current physical condition, but it felt good to do something useful around the house. But it definitely took its toll on me. I was exhausted and hurting. Just earlier in the week, I had learned I had a broken patella and a torn meniscus that had gone undiagnosed from my car wreck three months earlier. So now I was looking at another surgery. That would make six surgeries since November. Not really news I wanted to hear. Also, a few weeks back, the oil pump went out on Abby's Jeep, locking the motor up tighter than a drum. With a blown motor, it's pretty much a total loss, which wasn't really in our budget at that particular moment. But I have a friend who manages a car lot, and he found me a good deal on a super clean, like-new used vehicle for her.

So I was sitting in my chair, wallowing in self-pity and watching the Olympics while scrolling through Facebook. Every other post in my newsfeed seemed to be about the horrible school shooting in Florida. I had actually, and unfortunately, seen a video taken from inside the school, showing dead, bloodied bodies lying on the floor.

Innocent young people. Beautiful children. I didn't know it was going to be so graphic and was not expecting what I saw. It gave me goose bumps, and then tears welled up in my eyes. Those were someone's children. Someone's little girl. Someone's pride and joy. Someone's son who went to school, just like he did every day, but then never came home. My Lord.

I was feeling sorry for myself. And I didn't like that feeling. But it's hard. My body, although slowly healing from my accident, feels as though it's betraying me daily, by not being able to do the things I've taken for granted for so long. It hurts my pride. I've always been strong and tough, slowed down by very little. So this is humbling, and as hard as I try not to, I sometimes do feel sorry for myself. It's not a flattering look, I'm sure. But I'm human and I'm tired and I hurt and I'm mentally exhausted.

And in the same breath I looked over to see my girls. My healthy, safe girls. They weren't sick. They weren't hungry. They weren't burdened with heavy, unfair problems that many children in our country, and in others, have to deal with. They weren't lying dead on a white tile floor, in a classroom where they were just moments before laughing and talking with their friends and classmates. They weren't taking cover from a mentally deranged psycho who's just looking to cause pain. They were lying in their beds, watching stupid YouTube videos and laughing. Emma looked at me a little bit funny when I hugged her a little tighter and for a little longer than usual that night before bed. I realized that, yes, I've got my problems. My life isn't perfect. My family has all the same problems as any other family. But at the end of the day, there's really only one thing that matters to a parent. That truly matters. My kids are safe. They are healthy. They are warm and fed. And all of a sudden, my problems don't seem quite so bad. They're still problems, but they don't seem quite as heavy as they did before.

Right then and there, I closed my eyes and prayed sincere, heartfelt prayers for every person who was affected by the horrible, unnecessary, and pointless violence passed down by this domestic terrorist. I prayed that God would give those sitting at home that night—who were not as fortunate as I was, who were not listening to their children argue and laugh—a sense of peace and help them find some tranquility in this horrible tragedy. And then I thanked him for my beautiful, healthy family and asked for forgiveness for my selfishness. A sense of peace washed over me as I realized that although my problems do exist, I was safe in his hands, and everything was going to be all right after all. Amen.

Siblings

Y OUR BROTHER AND SISTER ARE the closest relations that you have in this world. You've got the same blood running through your veins. They should be your best friends." Good grief. How many times did I hear this growing up? Verbatim. Too many times to count. This is what my dad said to my brother, sister, and me each time we had an argument, a fight, or a disagreement of any kind. He said it. Every. Time. And I bet he laughs when he reads this, and he *will* read this, because he stalks my writing. He reads my Facebook page from my mom's Facebook page since he doesn't have one, and then he checks out the local paper's obituaries to see if he knows anyone who died. Every single day. He's a man of routine, which I love. He passed along that trait to me.

My sister is four years older than me, although she absolutely loves that I am generally thought to be the eldest of my siblings. And my little brother is six and a half years younger than me. So we are fairly well spread out. Yes, I am the middle child, to no one's surprise, I am sure. And there is a ten-and-a-half-year gap between my big sister and little brother. So, basically, every time my dad made the statement above, he was talking to me. It was either directed at me and my sister, or me and my brother. Because Shannon and Sky never fought. So I heard this. A lot.

My mom and dad did an excellent job of instilling in us a love of our siblings. We are all well into our adult lives now. Shannon has two fantastic boys with her amazing husband, Justin (who has been my brother now for longer than he wasn't), and my brother, Sky, and his lovely little bride, Ashley, have a little girl named Becka and a little boy named Hayes. April and I have our three girls, and we are all one, big, close-knit family. Shan and Sky are my best friends. If something good happens, I want to tell them. If something bad happens, I want to tell them. But like most brothers and sisters, this wasn't always the case. Things weren't always sunshine and rainbows.

Sure, I always loved them. And they were always my best friends. But sometimes I kind of wanted to kill them. Sometimes, probably even more often, they wanted to kill me. Or at least hit me really hard with something, in the face. Actually, they both did hit me really hard in the face, on more than one occasion. Sky hit me with an aluminum baseball bat while I was lying on the floor reading the comics in the paper, and also once with a curtain rod. Actually to be more accurate, he threw a curtain rod at me and stabbed it into the top of my head. He also came into the room once wearing his spurs, and only his spurs, and spurred me in my lower back. Which did not feel awesome.

And then one time Shannon was walking down a gravel driveway, barefoot, and for some reason I had a walking cane, and I thought it would be a really funny idea (and it was) to hook her ankle with the cane. But it made her step funny onto a rock and hurt her foot. She then wheeled around and brought a Butterbean-style haymaker from downtown, making solid contact, squarely in my eye socket. It even made a cool "punch" noise like on the *Dukes of Hazzard,* when they would punch people. My eye turned really black, and I told everyone at school that a horse kicked a pipe gate while I was closing it and it hit me in the face. I dang sure wasn't going to tell them that I had gotten my eye blacked out by my sister. To her credit, she did feel really bad about it as soon as it happened. I was a tough little turd, so even though it was a heck of a punch, it hurt my feelings way more than it hurt my eyeball.

There's a pretty good chance you have a brother or sister or both, or even a few of each. And there's also a good chance you have had a few fights, or maybe more than a few. I know, too, that sometimes siblings don't get along, and that makes me really sad for them. Because I know, regardless of anything I have ever done or any fight we may have ever had, that without fail, if I need my sister or if I need my brother, they'll be there. It is a very good feeling to know that no matter what kind of bonehead move you make—and I have made more than my fair share—they always have my back. No questions asked. Well, there may be a few questions, but they'll still do whatever I need from them. April says we are abnormal, because we all get along so well. But I love them. And I like them too. I can honestly say that as adults we have never had a fight or really even an argument. I guess we got that stuff out of our systems as kids.

So, as I watch Abby holding Gracee tonight, as I see her kissing her and telling her she loves her, I smile. And when I see Emma read Gracee a story before bedtime and Gracee's face lights up with happiness when she sees either of them, it makes me feel like we are, at least, doing one thing right. They are *great* big sisters. They love Gracee with all their might, and that just tickles me pink. For all three of them. I know they will always have each other.

No, they don't always get along. Sometimes they fight, and we even occasionally have a minor injury or two. But the other day, you know what I said to them when they were fighting? Yeah, you know what I said. I said, "Girls, your sisters are the closest relations that you have in this world. You've got the same blood running through your veins. They should be your best friends." Thanks, Dad.

My Twisted Road
to Fatherhood

A S YOU MAY KNOW BY NOW, I have the most beautiful five-year-old daughter on the face of the planet. Ever. My wife will tell you that Gracee has been equaled only on two other occasions in the history of mankind. I'm a very proud, embarrassingly overbearing papa. I can't imagine ever not wanting her.

But before I met her mother, I was quite adamant: "I'll never have kids. Period!" And I stuck to my guns for a long time. Friends, family, even strangers would overhear my declaration and say, "Oh, you *gotta* have kids! You just don't know what you're missing if you don't have kids! Life isn't worth living without kids!" Ugh. I *hated* that. I actually still hate it. Mainly because I didn't ask for their input. Being successful in my career was more than satisfying. However, as it turned out, their unwanted comments turned out to be true.

Here's the deal. When it came right down to it, the truth is I was completely terrified of kids. I didn't know how to talk to them. I didn't know what to do with them. My basic knowledge of children was this:

1. They're loud.
2. They're dirty.
3. They're really dirty.

And for those of you who don't know me, I grew up on a ranch, way out in the country, so I am no stranger to getting dirty. I do, however, have a rather large hang-up with "people germs." So when I say kids are dirty, I'm actually referring to boogers and snot and farts and pee and gross kid stuff like that.

But eventually I got the itch. That feeling. Some of you know what I'm talking about. That feeling when you look at a little girl sitting on her daddy's shoulders as he walks around, or when you see that little boy and his dad playing catch in the yard. "I think I want that." Wait, what did I just say?! *I think I want to be a dad.* Holy moly. I started to hyperventilate at just the thought of it. So when I told April I thought that maybe I kinda, sorta, wanted to, maybe, talk about having a baby, sorta, well, I'm not sure she knew what to say in return. So we didn't really "try," and we didn't really not try. Months came and went, and nothing. We didn't really talk about it. I'd taken a new job in Texas, and the girls were still in Oklahoma finishing up their school year. Life was busy, and April and I weren't trying, but we weren't not trying.

One morning April was acting really funny. She was being really quiet in both texts and on the phone, and I kept asking what was wrong, to which she replied, "Nothing." Okay. I know enough about women to know that when they say "nothing," it usually means "something." And I wasn't going to stop until I found out. I also had a pretty important meeting that day. I had to do a presentation to our CEO, CFO, VP, and to a boardroom full of others. The meeting was fairly long and boring, and I was still slyly texting her under the table trying to find out what the "nothing" was. Finally, she'd had enough of my nagging and texted a picture to me—a positive pregnancy test! She just sent a text. While I was in my meeting. With the CEO and thirty others. I was pretty new at this job, having only been there a few months. Men, temporary insanity is a real thing. I had an out-of-body experience. I heard nothing. My brain just went into a state of constant white noise. Stunned. Shocked. I had no brain activity. Only a dazed, blank stare.

Now, I'm losing my mind, y'all! My heart is racing at a rate that cannot be healthy. My hands are shaking. I've got goose bumps and I'm sweating. Still not paying the least bit of attention to the board meeting. That's when I hear, "You want to go ahead and give your opinion on this, Stoney?" *What?!* Is this a practical joke? Are there hidden cameras in the room? Surely they aren't talking to me right now. But I look up, with what I can only assume is the dazed and confused look of Forrest Gump being asked to do applied mathematics. I have *no idea* what they are talking about. I don't even know what *subject* we are talking about. I'm lost. I'm frazzled. I'm white as a ghost. And now I'm on the spot. Thirty sets of eyes bearing down on me. Unforgiving stares. It's a defining moment in my life, and I don't know what to say. Finally, I see some friendly eyes. *Oh yes, I know him! He's my friend!* I'm begging him with my eyes, *Please help me!* He understands and asks the question again! *Oh, thank you, sweet Jesus.* He asks me a question that even in my temporary mental state, I can answer, albeit stuttering and in run-on sentences. *I think I pulled it off!* I look around the room to semisatisfied faces. Heads are nodding like "Hey, this Stamper guy's really got it going on." *I did it!* I didn't get fired!

I look back down at my phone, still on the picture that had caused my near-death experience, and then it starts all over again. I'm going to have a *baby*! We made a human person! How crazy is that? I need to tell somebody. Anybody. I need to hug April. She's six hours away! An innumerable amount of questions and fears are running through my head, all at the same time.

And then I hear it again. "Stoney, why don't you go ahead and do your full presentation to the group." I'd be lying if I told you I remembered any part of that speech. I have no idea what I said. I'm going to assume I sped through at a pretty quick clip, but other than that, nothing, nada. At the completion of the meeting, the CEO, who happens to be my friend, says, "Dude, what in the world was that all about?" All I can do is show him the picture. He smiles from ear to ear and offers his congratulations.

Although I can't remember many things that were said that day, I will never forget the sequence of events that led up to the greatest thing I have ever had the opportunity to do. Be a daddy. But do your baby daddy a favor. And trust me on this. Don't rock his world until *after* his presentation. He'll appreciate it.

A House Is Not a Home

SEVERAL YEARS AGO, APRIL BOUGHT me a small sign for my office that reads "Never be so busy making a living that you forget to make a life." I can't imagine a more fitting adage for yours truly. I spent a dozen years doing precisely what that small wooden sign told me not to. I spent all my time, all my *life,* chasing the almighty dollar. I was so consumed with becoming successful that I never even realized my life was passing me by. But thankfully, one day April came along, bringing two little girls with her, and they changed my world. They changed everything I thought I knew about life. And they also introduced me to what would become my favorite simple pleasure—coming home.

Let me back up a little bit. I grew up in a great home. We were your normal little happy family of five from middle America. We had a three-bedroom, two-bath house just across the pasture from both sets of grandparents. Aunts, uncles, and cousins lined both sides of Murphy Road in both directions. We were a close family, and Murphy, Oklahoma, was our place.

It's funny what you remember from where you grew up. When I think of our little house, even though I haven't lived there in twenty years, I can still hear the screech of the woodstove doors as my dad loaded it up with firewood before we all went to bed. Sometimes, in the middle of the night, I'd hear my mom try to open the stove quietly so she could add more firewood without waking anyone up, but those doors weren't having it. They'd screech loudly, no matter how hard you tried to be quiet.

And if you went into the bedroom I shared with my brother, you could look at the trim around the doorframe and see how tall I grew every year from the time I was six years old. Nearly every good memory I have as a child happened in that house. No, in that *home*. My parents worked very hard to give us a happy home. And they nailed it. Looking back on it now, it wasn't the nicest house I'd ever been in. It had its quirks. It had this ugly blue linoleum in the kitchen and dining room for years. The toilet made some really funny sounds. And we didn't finish the back patio for a long time, so it had concrete blocks stacked up to the back door doubling as steps. The funny thing is, I didn't notice any of those things as a kid. I only notice them now, looking back. It never crossed my mind that it wasn't the nicest home in town, because, to me, it was perfect. My safe place.

My happy place. And still, to this day, when I think about my home, I think of that little brick house on Murphy Road.

I left that home for college in 1997, and other than a brief stint after college, I never really went back. I began my own journey and lived on my own. I lived in college dorms, a nice duplex on a golf course, an apartment on a lake, and then finally, I bought my first house. It was a small farm just around the corner from my parents and grandparents, a cute little house I was proud of. That year I also took a new job that required me to travel—a lot. It was not uncommon for me to be gone 250-plus days per year, a schedule not very conducive to any kind of home life. My "life" was spent in airports, hotels, and the driver's seat of rental cars. It wasn't long before I sold the farm and moved again. My next move found me in a beautiful condo on a Florida beach. From there, I moved to Richmond, Virginia. I bought a beautiful house in a little town outside of Richmond named Midlothian. It was in a great neighborhood with good people all around. The house was beautiful, and I was proud of it. But as I'm apt to do, after about five years there, I got the itch, packed up, and headed back to Oklahoma. Another beautiful house. But as with all the others, there was something missing. They were beautiful houses. I made many improvements on them, built new decks and patios, put in new tile floors. I *liked* the houses, but I never *loved* them. I never had the feeling that I had when I was in that little brick house on Murphy Road.

This is the point in my story when April and the girls come in. April and I had known each other since childhood, had reconnected, started dating, and then later decided to get married. April had two daughters, so I was now going to be a family man. And a good family man can't travel 250-plus days per year. So April and I discussed our options. I had an offer for a great job that would allow me to stay home, but it meant relocating—to Texas. After lots of talking and prayer, I took the new job in Texas. Yes, it was a terribly difficult decision to move our family, but ultimately, we felt it was best for us. April found us a new house, one with seven good acres, a four-stall barn with a tack room, and a nice-sized arena built out of solid pipe. That sounds great, huh? Well, yes and no. The house was a fixer-upper. Fences needed to be built, and the barn needed new siding. But once we were done with it, the value of the property doubled, at least. To us, it was worth the sacrifice.

For several years we put as much sweat equity as we could into that house, and it turned out pretty nice. At the very least, I stopped feeling embarrassed to have company over. But most important, it was in that house I began to sense the one thing I had been looking for, for more than twenty years. When I walked through the door at the end of a long workday, I set my briefcase down, and our youngest daughter, Gracee, would run to me with arms wide open. Abby and Emma would tell me funny stories about their day, and April would stand at the end of the line, waiting to give me a kiss and welcome me home. Man, there's no better feeling on this earth. And yes, that's right. I said *home.*

Life in a Small Town

I GREW UP IN THE SMALL TOWN of Locust Grove in northeast Oklahoma. Last time I checked, the population was around fifteen hundred people, and I doubt that has increased much over the years. Picture in your mind a small rural community. You'll likely envision a narrow main street lined with some barber shops and beauty salons, a burger joint that serves some of the world's best ice cream, a bank, an insurance agent's office, and probably an auto mechanic's shop or two. You've pretty much just described Locust Grove to a tee. Quaint, friendly, nosy, helpful, caring, and supportive. You like how I snuck *nosy* in there?

I love my hometown. Most of my favorite memories in life go back to that little town. From the annual Founder's Day Parade, where the whole town showed up to celebrate with live music, old cars, and Indian tacos, to Charlie's In-N-Out store, where I would walk to buy candy or a Dr Pepper in a real glass bottle. Charlie knew the name of every person in town, and watching him expertly flip the coins into the air from the cash register to give you your change made him epically cool. On to Twin Bridges that crossed Spring Creek, where the water was so painfully cold that you couldn't breathe for nearly ten minutes after jumping in. And then Low Water Dam, where we'd steal away as teenagers to build bonfires. And on occasion we'd drive out even farther to Phillip's Lounge, where we'd pick up the dad of one of our friends, a dad who'd had a few too many drinks. It's like that line from "Small Town," the song John Mellencamp made famous: "No, I cannot forget where it is that I come from."

Looking back on my childhood, there are so many great things about growing up in a small community. But as a kid, especially as a teenager, it didn't always feel like a good thing. Especially if you were a kid who tended to get into mischief, which I just happened to be. Secrets in small towns tend to spread like wildfire. Everyone knows everyone. Everyone is usually kin, either by blood or by marriage. If you want to do something you don't want your mama to know about, you'd best go out of town to do it. Even better, completely out of the county—and even then, there are no guarantees that your secret is safe. I once got a little out of control in Oolagah, Oklahoma, over an hour away from home, and my mama knew about it before I got back to the house. My second-grade teacher was my dad's high school girlfriend. My Future Farmers of America (FFA) instructor was my dad's best friend since childhood. This was way back when a teacher could paddle you without giving it a second thought. And I certainly got my fair share of paddlings. There was an unwritten understanding between my parents and the school. If a Stamper kid needs some licks, spank his butt. My FFA instructor took this very literally. And he enjoyed it. He would call my dad in the evenings at home, and they would laugh about it. It's hard to imagine this happening these days, even at a small school like Locust Grove.

When I graduated high school, I headed to Miami, Oklahoma, to attend Northeastern Oklahoma A&M College. After two years there, I moved on to Stillwater, Oklahoma, so I could fulfill my dream of becoming an Oklahoma State Cowboy. After college, I begrudgingly went back to the ranch for a couple of years, but I wanted something different. Something bigger. Something more exciting than what little old Locust Grove could provide. I wanted to get out of the town that only had Ranch House Pizza, Cook's Restaurant, Country Cottage, or Jerry's Dari-Ette as dining options. I didn't want to have to drive an hour to go to a real city where I could shop in real stores, eat at real restaurants, or watch a real movie. I wanted *more*. I knew something more important, more real was waiting for me out there somewhere.

In 2004 I got my chance. A friend of mine had just bought a new manufacturing company in the Florida Panhandle. He called and asked to meet up to discuss my working for him. I discussed it with my dad, who wasn't very excited at the prospect of my moving that far away from him, so we decided to price myself high. If my friend wanted me bad enough to pay some big bucks, then I'd gladly take them. So I sat down with my friend, told him what it would take to get me to move everything I owned, and my dog, to Navarre

Beach, Florida. I named my price, and he quickly asked when I could start. *Hot dang,* I thought. *It's really going to happen. I'm leaving Locust Grove, finally.* My parents, brother, sister, and her family waved goodbye as I drove away.

Remember in the opening scene of *Perfect Strangers* when Balki Bartokomous gets on the wagon headed for New York? It was kind of like that. Except I was in a truck and not a horse-drawn wagon. And I'm not from Mypos. But like Balki, I was setting out on my journey. I was going out to find whatever it was that had been calling to me for all those years. So I pointed that Dodge truck east and headed toward Florida. It was a very surreal feeling, leaving everything I had ever known, every comfort, headed toward a town in the Panhandle of Florida where I did not know a single solitary person. I felt excited by the prospect of living somewhere new, seeing new things, meeting new people. A real life. But I also felt something else, something I didn't expect. Even though I was so excited about the adventure that lay ahead of me, I also felt an unexpected hint of sadness, although I wasn't exactly sure why. I was where I wanted to be. I was doing what I wanted to do.

Fast forward about fourteen years, and I still haven't made it back home to Locust Grove, although I'm certainly closer now than when I lived in Florida. Having a wife and kids now, I'm responsible for raising girls. They go to a good school in Texas, but it's big. Instead of forty to sixty kids in their grade, they now have four hundred. It's minutes away from the nicest restaurants, the best shopping, and a half-dozen movie theaters. There are a lot of people in town that I don't know. Heck, I don't know most of them. And even though the convenience of living in a bigger city is definitely a plus, I find myself wishing for my girls the small town life that April and I had the privilege of growing up with. That's right. I said *privilege*. But there's a verse in the Bible about getting everything you want but losing yourself. I understand that verse now.

When Mama's Gone

$\mathcal{S}$OME PEOPLE JUST SEEM BORN to be parents. They just fall effortlessly into the parenting routine as though they've been doing it all their lives. The feeding, burping, diaper changing, bathing, and getting these tiny little people dressed in their itsy-bitsy, impossible onesies with buttons, zippers, and flaps out the wazoo can be unbelievably overwhelming. Yet some of these *superparents* seem to perform these daily challenges as easily as Simone Biles doing a cartwheel.

I was not one of these people. I was thirty-three years old when Gracee June was born, and since she is my only biological child, I had never tackled even one of those previously mentioned parental duties before March 29, 2013. Gracee came along and I was lost. Scared.

Confused. You name it, I didn't know how to do it, any of it. But as time went on, I changed countless diapers and made thousands of bottles, and soon I became a fairly able-bodied caregiver for my little munchkin. But it wasn't without some major speed bumps. There were days when I wondered if God second-guessed himself when he thought I could one day be a dad.

One of those days occurred on May 16, 2013. Yes, I remember the exact date. I relive the whole scene in my mind often. It was the Thursday after Mother's Day, and for her special day I bought April a spa package at a local salon. She was to be pampered with a manicure, pedicure, and massage. The whole works. It was completely her day. Gracee was only six weeks old, and for the very first time I was going to keep her at home, all by myself. You caught that last phrase, right—"all by myself"?

From day one, Gracee and I have had this amazing connection. I have always felt that I could look at her face and see exactly what she was thinking. Seriously, like the two of us are on some other wavelength. So, on that special first day together, my six-week-old daughter and I began having a conversation. We were lying on the couch, and she looked at me with questioning eyes, and I'm convinced it went something like this:

Gracee: "Hey, Daddy. Where's Mama?"

Me: "Well, she's getting her Queen-for-the-Day spa treatment that you and your sisters gave her for Mother's Day."

Gracee: "Oh, well, that's cool. Thank you for watching me today while she goes and does that. She really deserves it.

Oh, and, Daddy? There's just one more thing that I wanted to say to you . . ."

And then Gracee projectile vomited straight up into the air.

It was astonishing, like a puke fountain at the Bellagio. It covered her face and hair and eyes. It was in her ears, all over her clothes, and all over my clothes and arms. The volume was impressive considering she'd only eaten about four ounces. At this point, I jumped up and got her to the bedroom to start getting that stuff off her face and hair. I took her clothes off, wrapped her up, and headed to the kitchen for our first solo bath. I figured I could do this. I'd seen April do it dozens of times. So I placed her on a towel on the counter, and she was all happy and smiley. And for a few seconds there, I truly thought everything was going to be okay. I really did.

I started clearing breakfast dishes out of the sink while I held my hand on Gracee's belly so she wouldn't roll off the counter. And then my sweet six-week-old daughter began communicating with me again, what I refer to in retrospect as the "Hey, Daddy" deluge.

Gracee: "Hey, Daddy, what's this little plastic rack with all my bottles on it? I think I'll throw it so all the bottles and nipples loudly crash on the floor. Hey, Daddy, all those bottles flying around and banging off the tile floor for no apparent reason? They just scared me really bad, so I'm going to scream real loud now for a while."

Me: "No, baby, don't scream. Please don't scream. I'm just trying to get the water to the right temperature for you. Please don't scream."

Gracee proceeded to scream her lungs out. Finally, the water was dialed to the right temperature, so I peeled her diaper off, picked her up, and proceeded to ease her down into the water. But then, at the last second, I decided that the water was a tad too warm, so I held on to her and tried to cool it down just a bit.

Gracee: "Hey, Daddy? I've really got to pee."

And then she peed, all over my T-shirt and belly. I quickly set her down into her little bath chair thingy and started running the warm water over her. She smiled so pretty at me.

Gracee: "Hey, Daddy? I *love* baths. They make me so
   relaxed. I think I'll go ahead and make a poop."
Me (pleading again): "Please, Gracee, no!" (But like that
   Ray Stevens song about Ethel and the streak, it was too
   late.)
Gracee: "Hey, Daddy? I feel much better."

To make a long story just a bit shorter, I grabbed the three different kinds of baby soap by the sink and, just to be safe, we used all three of them. I scrubbed her up really good—lather, wash, rinse, repeat, and then we were done. I looked around. We survived. No one was hurt, nothing broken that couldn't be fixed. Yeah, that's right, easy as pie.

Gracee: "Hey, Daddy? You did good."

I felt deep within my bones that I pulled out a win. A huge win. Then, with a smug look of victory on my face, I glanced over at the clock on the wall. April had only been gone thirty minutes. She wouldn't be home for at least another three and a half hours.

Gracee: "Hey, Daddy? . . ."

The Only Certainty

I T WAS A GORGEOUS SPRING EVENING in East Texas, and my little family was enjoying our first taste of nonwinter weather in months. The temperature was perfect, there was a gentle breeze coming out of the north, and the sun was beginning to slowly sneak down behind the trees in our backyard. I was having one of those moments. You know what I'm talking about. One of those moments when everything in life just feels perfect. Everything was in its place. I had no stress about work, no worries about money, nor was I fretting over the long list of things that needed to be done around the house. Instead, something very uncommon occurred. Something that is truly very rare in my life. I was at peace. I felt calm. My busy, crazy, anxious mind found a brief moment of wonderful solace.

I looked around proudly at my family and my home. The older girls, Abby and Emma, were running through the green clover in the pasture chasing each other and laughing as their mother watched, smiling from the porch swing. Then my gaze focused on my beautiful blue-eyed toddler, Gracee. Only a few weeks had passed since her second birthday, and she is the apple of her daddy's eye. A true sight to behold. Gracee's eyes caught mine and she smiled, and then in the most adorable southern belle voice I've ever heard, she said, "Hi, Daddy." And just like that, my heart nearly burst wide open. How could I be so lucky to be blessed with this life? Why in the world did the good Lord see fit to give me this little piece of paradise?

Then, as if Gracee could hear those peaceful thoughts running through my head, I watched helplessly as she raised a chubby little hand to her lips and, staring me dead in the eyes, put a big, fresh, wet pile of chicken poop into her cherubic mouth. Panic quickly replaced my blissful serenity. "Gracee, *nooooo*!" I yelled. But I was too late. The damage had been done. I stared at her blankly, in shock at what she'd just done. She grinned at me, smacked her lips a few times, giggled, spit what remained into her hands, and instantly wiped it on her shirt. She then looked at me and said, "*Eeeewwww*, Gracee. No, no!" After all that, she laughed and laughed as she walked away, as though absolutely nothing out of the ordinary had just happened.

I wish I could say that was the first time something like that had happened. But that would be a lie. A big lie. Because the truth of the matter is something like this seems to occur on a near-daily basis. Countless times in the last seven years have I been completely horrified by something I've seen or heard these girls do.

Having lived a long time with no children, I led a very clean, neat life. I tended to be fairly uptight, and according to my nephew Joby, "Stone's got lots of rules." But that was then, and this is now. And "now" is a house filled with girls and their beautiful mother and hair bows, cheerleading, bobby pins, smelly shoes, and science projects. In a baptism of fire, I was forced to learn what it means to be a parent. My approach to life is always be a student, always be learning. So I read every parenting article I could find online and pored through countless books on the subject. Topics included "How to be a good *step*father and earn their trust" and "Teaching your kids to be well mannered and kind and confident." Tall orders, huh?

But it was Albert Einstein who once said, "The only source of knowledge is experience." And I have found that to be especially true when it comes to being a parent. No matter how hard you try, some things just simply cannot be learned without experience. Sometimes things happen and absolutely nothing in the parenting manuals, articles, or videos will ever prepare you for that moment, like when your one-year-old daughter smooshes an entire plate of refried beans and rice in her hair. Or when she breaks wind in a restaurant and informs the entire restaurant of what just happened.

The only certainty I've come across in parenting is that you never know what's going to happen next. Parenting is one big pile of uncertainty, so to speak. And once you're done being disgusted, flabbergasted, and/or embarrassed, you'll usually smile quietly to yourself and think, *Wow, I never saw that coming.*

I Fought the Mall,
and the Mall . . .

'M A GOOD GIFT GIVER. I'm not bragging or anything. I'm just saying, I'm amazing, maybe the best ever. Maybe that's bragging a little. But I pay close attention to the things the recipient of my gift wants, and then I plan and shop for the best deal, well ahead of the special day. It's a wonderful, thoughtful process.

No, no, no. That entire first paragraph is a big fat lie. I don't do any of that stuff. I wouldn't say I'm the worst gift giver in the world, but I definitely leave a lot to be desired. I may have an idea of what someone may like, but there's no way I plan it out early. And I'm just as likely to pay double what something's worth than shop early and get a good deal.

Of course, when it's the day before your wife's birthday and you've got nothing, worries about cost go straight out the window. Your only focus is having a good gift for her birthday. Four hundred dollars for a purse? Sold! I can't speak for all men, but I'd gladly pay four hundred dollars to stay out of the doghouse. But maybe that's just me.

My wife's birthday is February 11. And the older two of my three daughters, Abby and Emma, wanted to give Mom their own presents, ones they picked out, in a store you have to drive to, and neither of them could drive. Now, I'd rather get in a bare-knuckle bar brawl with Mike Tyson, circa 1985, than go to the mall. But that particular year I'd put it off as long as I could. So on the day before April's birthday, as much as it pained me to do it, I picked the girls up from school and, with the bravery and courage of a kamikaze pilot, headed to the mall.

Excitement oozed from their pores as we pulled into the parking lot. There was nonstop giggling and talking. "Dad is taking us to the mall! This is so much fun! We're going to spend all his money!" As we walked in from the parking lot, I established the ground rules. "Okay, girls. Stay together. Do *not* run off by yourselves. We aren't here to shop for *you*. Let's find some presents your mom will like, buy them, and get out of here as quickly as possible. We all clear? Okay. Ready. Break!"

Before we even got into the main section of the mall where all the stores were, I could tell my ground rules were going to be very hard to enforce. Emma took off at a near run. "*Emma!* Get back here!" I screamed, as she headed directly into a fancy jewelry store. I had nightmarish visions of broken glass and thousands of dollars of damage as my energetic little blond-haired tornado whirled around from one display to the next. I rushed in and escorted her out. "Emma," I said. "*Don't* run off!" She was completely unfazed by my instructions and headed off in another direction. Abby, although older and calmer, looked like a racehorse just before the gates open. I gathered them together in front of the food court to reestablish my ground rules and make a plan.

Unfortunately, I chose to do this right in front of Cinnabon. As I was talking, I noticed Emma was having a hard time paying attention. "Emma, are you listening?" I asked. She replied, "Can I *please* have an Oreo chocolate chip diabetic energy explosion?" (Okay, that's not really what she called it, but it was something like that.) My knee-jerk reaction was a resounding "No!" But then they teamed up on me. "Pretty please, can *we* have one?" The flutter of long eyelashes and adorable smiles got the better of me. To put on a smidge of authority, I said, "Girls, you don't need one of those. They're big and expensive, and we're going to eat dinner when we're done here." But as you might guess, that was all for nothing. They knew they were getting the two-thousand-calorie milkshake before the words even left my mouth.

So I'd spent fourteen dollars already, and we'd yet to actually do any shopping. It was high time to get down to business. "Where do we need to go first, girls?" I asked.

"Let's go into Journeys!" they yelled.

"Girls, Journeys only has clothes for girls. Your mom is turning thirty-three years old tomorrow. I doubt there's anything in there she'll want." But much like the milkshake moment, my authority and opinion were ignored, and we journeyed into Journeys.

"Girls, remember. *We are shopping for your mother!*" They giggled at each other and continued looking at clothes—for themselves. Yes, I was being taken advantage of and realized the only way out of there was with brute force. So I rounded them up and marched them through the doors, both of them looking back over their shoulders. "Hey, there's the Sunglass Hut. There's a pair of Coach sunglasses your mom's been wanting. Let's go look over there." The girls were about as excited as if I had just asked them to go do their math homework. I found the ones I was pretty sure April wanted, so I asked Abby for her opinion. She was thirteen at the time, and pretty fashionable. She was also kind of hormonal, and pouting because I'd just embarrassed her by dragging her out of Journeys. I asked again, "What do you think of these?" as I held up the sunglasses. She responded with a less than ecstatic "I dunno." I said, "What do you mean? These are cool. I think she'll like them. I'm pretty sure these are the ones she wants." Abby said, "I don't like them. I don't think she will like them." Only seconds ago, I had been pretty confident about the glasses. Now my confidence was wavering. "You don't think she will like them?" I was deflated. I thought I had done so well. Abby shrugged. "I'm going to go in Claire's." Emma screamed *"Yes!"* and away they flew.

Well, what now? I didn't really want to go the gift card route, but I also didn't want to spend a couple hundred bucks on a pair of sunglasses April wouldn't like. So with a bruised ego, I bought a gift card and made my way into Claire's, where the girls were again abuzz with energy, gazing at the wonderland of hair bows, earrings, necklaces, headbands, and bracelets. On one hand, most of that stuff is cheap. On the other hand, it's mostly a bunch of glittery, sparkly trinkets. I found the girls, each with their own shopping baskets, full of wonderful things they'd selected for their mom. I didn't think any of it looked like anything April would like. It looked like stuff that nine- and thirteen-year-old girls like. I smelled a conspiracy. But in the daily classroom of "learning to be a dad," I've learned not to argue about it. We got the gift card for the sunglasses, and the girls each had several things to give their mom, just from them.

Hallelujah! The end was in sight. I thought I might just survive the mall after all. I ran a half marathon once, and that was just how I felt when I could see the finish line. My heart was racing. I was filled with adrenaline. My confidence was soaring. And then, as it usually does when Emma and I are involved, disaster struck. Emma dropped her seven-dollar milkshake. It landed hard on the tile floor, and the cup split in half, exploding all over the floor and racks of merchandise. I jerked spastically to try to catch it, and when I did, I knocked over a rack of headbands, sending them scattering across the floor. The lid flew off the cup, and cold, sticky milkshake managed to cover anything and everything in a ten-foot radius. That included me, Emma, and a nice lady who just happened to be standing a little too close.

I looked around apologetically to anyone who would make eye contact. I snapped into action, grabbed some paper towels, and made a miserable attempt to clean up the horrible mess we'd just created. I gave a handful of paper towels to the unlucky but nice lady standing near us and apologized profusely. I paid for our things, quickly, and got the heck out of there before we tore anything else up.

I was then in as big of a hurry to get out of the mall as the girls were to get into the mall when we first arrived. Emma was behind me, trying to keep up, and she suddenly yelled, "Wait! We need to go to Build-A-Bear!"

I said, "Emma, your mother does *not* want anything from Build-A-Bear. I'm sure of it."

"Well, she probably doesn't want any of this junk we got her at Claire's either, but we still got it for her!"

That is a very good point, Em. Sorry, April. Better luck next year.

The Art of Stepparenting

I F YOU'RE READING THIS, then there's a pretty good chance you are a parent, were at one time a parent, or you'd love to be one someday. That being said, there's also a pretty good chance you are a stepparent. According to the Stepfamily Foundation and the US Bureau of Census, there are at least thirty million children in the USA alone living with one biological and one nonbiological parent. That's a lot of families—and a lot of confused little kids—having to learn to live with, and trust, someone who is not their "real" mom or dad. It also makes for, in my case anyway, some very confused stepparents.

First off, if you are a stepparent, let me tip my hat to you and say "Thank you." You deserve it. Knowing there are millions of others out there, losing their minds, struggling with some of the same "you're not my dad" issues I was going through daily, gave me a certain amount of confidence. It's an "if they can do it, I can do it" kind of thing. I don't think I am any better than anyone else, but I don't think I am necessarily any worse, either.

I have two beautiful "step" daughters. That's what the law calls them. I just call them my daughters. My girls. They are no less my daughters than my biological daughter, Gracee. I love them, and I would do anything for either one of them. However, it's been a long, screwy ride to get where we are today. April still laughs at how uncomfortably I acted the first day I met Abby and Emma. I am a fairly capable person. I can generally handle myself adequately, and with confidence, in nearly any situation. Very few things can make me shake in my boots. But *that* day. That day I was as nervous as a long-tailed cat in a room full of rocking chairs. I couldn't sit still. I was up and down, walking around. A jittery mess. I was terrified. The gravity of the situation, to me, was crushing. Afterward, I realized I was nervous on many different levels.

First, apparently this awesome, beautiful woman that I really liked a lot liked me so much she wanted me to meet her kids. That, in itself, made me get a little shaky. Oh, and she had never introduced a man to her kids before. To me, that screamed commitment, which made me feel like there was a cable clamp around my esophagus. But then I began to think about other things. Like, *Okay, I really like her. Love her, even.* (Gulp.) *But what if her kids don't like me? Will she still want to date me? That's heavy.* Talk about pressure! I'd had a hard enough time trying to get one woman to like me for any extended period of time, much less three! And what if I didn't like them?! I know that sounds a little harsh, because they were just little girls, but let's be honest: some people are kid people and some aren't. I never had been. Ever. So the thought of really liking April, and the possibility of these kids jacking everything up, was a pretty legitimate fear. And even though others may not admit it, I know I am not the only one who has felt that way.

Abby and Emma are quite different from each other. In fact, they couldn't be more opposite. First, we've got Emma—a blonde with bright blue eyes. She is spirited and wild. The next thing that will come out of her mouth? Well, your guess is just as good as mine. I'd calculate that about 60 percent of the actual words that come out of her mouth probably make their way onto my blog—*The Daddy Diaries*. If you happen to have an itch to write a daddy blog, well, Emma is a stinkin' gold mine. I have to write down the funny things she says because she says them so often, I'll forget them if I don't. She's also very outgoing, very loving, and very easy to get to know. She'll talk to anyone and will tell you all about herself in the first ten minutes you meet her. Not long after we met, she would sit on my lap, give me a hug when I would leave, and when she first told me she loved me, I thought I might pass completely out. As far as making me feel comfortable, Emma did great.

Then we've got Abby—a brunette with hazel eyes. And definitely a tougher nut to crack. She has an excellent, very dry sense of humor. She is quiet, calm, and mature for her age, and extremely laid back. Now, don't get me wrong. She is completely capable of going off the rails of the crazy train, but she is also very cautious. She and her mom have quite the unique relationship, and when I first came along, Abby was scared I was going to somehow affect that. She wasn't necessarily mean to me, but she was totally and completely indifferent to my existence. She would act like I wasn't in the room. She refused to look at me and would only speak to me in muted, one-syllable words, and then only if her mother made her. She made me *so nervous.*

It became my mission in life to make her like me. I mean, c'mon, everyone likes me. Well, almost. So surely I could make this little girl, ten years old at the time, like me. I was determined to make this happen. I tried being sweet. Nope. Not even close. I tried being funny. Nope. She'd go out of her way not to laugh. I tried buying her things, to which she would say "Thank you," because she has good manners, but nothing seemed to crack through her shell. For months I tried and tried, and I didn't seem to make any progress whatsoever. It began to really upset me, although I did my best to not let Abby know it. April did try to make me feel better about it, but I was at a loss. She said, "Just ignore her. She'll come around eventually." But that was impossible. I couldn't make myself ignore her. So I just kept trying.

And then one day she came and sat down by me on the couch . . .

And then she told me a story of something funny that happened at school . . .

And then she laughed about it and said, "Isn't that funny?"

And then one night she asked me if I'd take her to Sonic to get her some ice cream . . .

What I am getting at is that she finally began to trust me, a little at a time. She realized I wasn't there to steal her mother away from her. Or to steal her things or kill her dog. She realized I just genuinely loved her mom but that I also genuinely loved her. She realized my attitude toward her wasn't an act but it was who I really was and how

I really felt. I was there because I wanted to be. Not because I had to be. And finally, it *worked*!

So if you've been lucky enough, as I was, to inherit some children from a previous relationship, and you're slamming your head into a wall or something, just hang in there. Just keep showing them that you are there for the long haul. Be nice to them; try not to be too awkward or uncomfortable like I was, because that probably ain't gonna help a whole lot. But if I could only give you one solid piece of advice, here it is: The most important thing you can do, by far, is show them you really love their mother (or father). Once they see that and believe it, I promise you those kids will fall in line. I truly believe that. Now, I know some of you will have a harder time with this than others, but perseverance is the key. The King James Bible calls it *longsuffering*. But yes, *perseverance* sounds a little more upbeat.

Now, don't get me wrong, we are still very much a work in progress. We continue to have our days when we all want to clobber each other. But that's how family goes. And perseverance is the key.

Buckle Up, Dad

HEY (I'M NOT SURE WHO "THEY" are exactly) say confession is good for the soul. All right then, here goes. I am a control freak. There, I said it. It feels good to get that out in the open. I like to be the boss. Scratch that. I *need* to be the boss. I make the decisions. If something needs to be done, I do it. Not in a chauvinistic Ike Turner kind of way. Just an "I've got to take care of my family" kind of way. It's an inherent characteristic that's built into my DNA, just like the ancient cavemen clubbing saber-toothed tigers to protect their young, although there really aren't too many saber-toothed tigers running around these days. Not in East Texas, anyway.

My control freakishness has been a relatively good asset to my career. I've always been a go-getter who got things done. I'm good at managing my time, and I'm good at prioritizing. I'm exceedingly good at handling upset people and making them feel good and important and calming them down. I'm a voice of reason, logic, and a problem solver. For the most part, I'm respected and well thought of, minus the rare occasion when I feel the need to bluntly set things straight or simply cut ties with someone, which I am not opposed to doing when necessary. Work is relatively easy for me. I'm just kind of built for it.

But until seven years ago, my job was really all that needed managing in my life. I was single with no kids (sounds weird, huh?), so my home life was pretty simple. But then I met April, and she had Abby and Emma, and then a couple years later we had Gracee, and my whole world turned upside down. I soon learned a very important and painful lesson: I may be the boss at work, but I'm not the boss at home. I like to think I am, of course, but the truth is, a flutter of their eyelashes, a pretty smile, plus throw in a hug and I'll do just about anything they ask. Usually it's fairly small. Take them to the store. Help them with their homework. Help them with their FFA projects. All things I can generally handle without too much problem. But here lately, there's been another task added to my fatherly duties, and for the first time, I am not 100 percent sure I am up for the task. For a control freak like me, this is the ultimate test. Nothing, and I repeat *nothing,* is quite so humbling and frightening as relinquishing control of your motor vehicle to your fifteen-year-old daughter. Never in my thirty-eight years of life has it been so difficult to sit idly by and watch someone else do something. And in *my* truck? You've got to be kidding me!

Unfortunately, this is my new reality. My daughter will be old enough to drive soon, and I can either teach her the right way to do it or pay for lots of repairs and an insurance premium that keeps reaching for the stars. So even though my heart was screaming *No!* my brain was telling me I had no choice. I started Abby off slowly, letting her drive around the pasture. I'd watch as she made slow, lazy circles around the field, and occasionally she'd throw it in reverse and try to back up to something (usually it was unsuccessful). Because I'm old, I didn't have to take drivers' education classes, but since it's mandatory now where we live, April and I got her enrolled. I had this crazy idea that when she was done with her three-week class, she'd be a knowledgeable and competent driver. Boy, was I wrong. So wrong. I'm not really sure what she learned in there, except that a red octagonal-shaped sign means *stop*. The class did do one thing, though—it made her feel much smarter.

She became a worse backseat driver than her mother. "Stoney, you're following too close!" "Stoney, you're speeding!" "Oh my gosh, Stoney, you totally just ran that red light!" That got old, and fast. But still, even after the class, she had no real experience behind the wheel.

That training, my friends, fell on me.

Abby in the driver's seat of my truck. Me in the passenger seat, sweating bullets. "Okay now, put on your seatbelt. Adjust your seat and mirrors. Okay now, put it in reverse, and back out slowly. *Slowly! I said SLOWLY!*" That was me before we'd even backed out of the driveway, and she was already going too fast. But then, once we got on the road, she was going way too slow.

"Okay, go a little faster. Whoa, okay, a little slower. Get back in your lane! *Oh my gosh, Abby! Stay in your lane!*" Then she screamed back, *"Stop yelling! You're making me nervous!"* And so I replied, "Well, you're making me nervous!"

We made a loop around town, zigzagging down the road at thirty miles per hour in a sixty-five-mile-per-hour zone and then sixty-five miles per hour in a thirty-mile-per-hour zone, changing lanes without checking the mirrors and not using blinkers. We took a back road that would lead us back to the house with less traffic. As we approached our road, she didn't seem to be slowing down.

I said, "Your turn is coming up." But still she maintained her speed. I repeated myself. "Hey, your turn is coming up. Hey! You're going to miss the turn!" And just when I thought she'd surely miss the ninety-degree turn from Blackjack Road, she turned the wheel hard, without ever touching the brakes. Of course, we were going too fast and our momentum wouldn't allow us to make the turn. She slammed the brakes, but into the far ditch we went, missing the on-coming stop sign by inches. We both sat silent for a moment. I think we were both reflecting on our lives and thankful to still be among the living.

I looked at her. She looked at me. And then she said, "I was going too fast." Yeah. No joke, kid.

After a few more months of practice, her driving improved and, thankfully, the ditch incident is the closest we came to a fiery crash. But here's the good news. I've learned that yelling and stomping on the imaginary brake pedal in the floorboard from the passenger side might feel good in the moment, but it does no good in the long drive. I've learned to take deep breaths and give constructive criticism rather than scream bloody murder and duck for cover. I am proud of her for becoming a better driver, but secretly, I may be a little prouder that I've learned it's okay to hand over the reins to someone else, even if it's just for a bit. Even if I'm handing them over to a teenager.

They (again, who is "they"?) say you can't teach an old dog new tricks. And they may be right. But I'm living proof you can teach an old control freak who is suddenly a new dad a thing or two.

Go Down Swingin'

I GRIPPED THE BAT TIGHTLY in my hands. Too tightly. I wrung my hands back and forth in anxiousness as I watched the pitcher check first base, then turn his focus toward the little freckled kid at home plate—that would be me. He wound up and fired the ball. I gripped the bat a tad tighter and then did nothing as the ball flew over the plate and smacked into the catcher's mitt. "Strike two!"

My shoulders slumped. I backed out of the box and turned to look at my dugout. My coach, Dickie Willis, was my best friend's dad. Coach treated me just like his own. "Swing the bat, Stoney!"

I stepped back in the batter's box. Again, I raised my eyes to the pitcher. I watched him check the runner on first base, then wind up, and then pitch. And once again, I did nothing. I heard the ball hit the glove. I heard the umpire yell, "Strike three!" I walked slowly, defeated, back to the dugout. With tears in my eyes, I looked up at my coach. He shook his head and said, "If you don't swing the bat, kid, you won't ever hit the ball." I had disappointed my coach and my team. I nodded my head in recognition and found myself a place on the bench.

On the surface that sounds like basic baseball advice. I mean, it's pretty simple, right? If you swing the bat, you've got at least a chance to hit the ball. If you don't swing the bat, there's no chance. You don't have to be Babe Ruth to figure that one out.

After the game, I got in the truck with my dad. "You played well tonight, Stone. You made a great catch in center field, and you did a good job backing up second base." Dad was always positive, and he did his best to build my confidence and focus on the positive points of my performance. Only after he had patted my back and made me laugh and smile would he venture off into the things he felt needed work. But even then, he was always kind. I sensed he was getting ready to start talking about the places I needed to improve, so I decided to beat him to the punch.

"I'm not a good batter, Dad. I struck out. I always strike out." He didn't say anything for a minute. He just let my words hang in the air between us. But then he spoke, and when Dad spoke, I always tried to listen closely. "Whether or not you are a good batter isn't really in question here, Stone. I have no doubt that if you really tried to be a good batter, you would be. But here's what I am seeing. You're not trying. When you don't take a swing at the ball, you are accepting defeat without even giving any effort."

We sat in silence for a few moments; then he asked, "Why aren't you swinging at the ball?" I thought about the question for a bit and finally replied, "He was throwing really hard, and I guess I was just afraid I would miss it." What my dad said next was undoubtedly one of those moments when everything becomes clear, when something in your mind clicks.

Dad said, "Well, let me ask you. Would you feel just as bad right now if you had swung at the ball but still missed it? Either way, you struck out. But would you rather swing and miss? Or would you rather just not try?"

At that precise moment, I knew whom I'd most disappointed—myself. Not for striking out, but for not trying to hit the ball at all. Dad's simple piece of advice changed who I was. I made my mind up right that second. I'd never lose for lack of effort. From that point forward, I tried with all my might at everything I did. I wasn't the best athlete at the school, but I tried hard. I wasn't the best student either, but I tried hard. I never wanted to feel that disappointment in myself again. I never wanted to feel like I could've given more but just didn't try.

In a very real sense, I am who I am today because of that one simple talk I had with my dad in his old red Ford pickup on the seven-mile drive home from a baseball game more than twenty-five years ago. I remember it like it was yesterday.

But fast-forward. Now I'm a thirtysomething dad myself. My daughter Emma is the second baseman for her softball team, and she reminds me of myself in so many ways. I am her coach at third base, and she is stepping into the batter's box, facing a pitcher who throws faster and harder than any other girl in our league.

I watch Emma as she grips the bat and wrings it in her hands. I can see the anxiety in her face. I'm mumbling beneath my breath, "Swing the bat, baby. Just swing the bat." The pitcher winds up and delivers a fastball right down the middle. "Strike!" I see her slump. I holler at her from third base, "Swing the bat, Em! You can do it! You've got to swing at it!" We make eye contact, and she nods her head at me. She steps back into the box, digs her feet in, and gets set. She's got a different look on her face now. She's focused. She's determined. The pitcher winds up and fires a harder, faster pitch at her. This time, she swings. There's the distinctive sound of a ball hitting an aluminum bat—sort of a *thwink*. The crowd begins to cheer as Emma starts to run toward first base. But then the ump screams, "Foul ball!" The ball had just caught the tip of her bat and flew maybe fifteen feet up the first-base line. Her mother and I clap and yell as if she'd hit a grand slam. "You've got her speed down now, Em! Just straighten the next one out. You got it."

Again, she gets ready for the pitch. The count is 0–2. The pitcher throws the ball. Emma steps with her left leg and slings the bat in front of her, just like she's been taught. She rotates her hips and swings through the ball with all her little seventy-five-pound frame. And the ball hits the catcher's mitt. "Strike three!" Her shoulders sink as she wilts out of the batter's box and heads back toward me. I prepare myself for tears, but what I get is something else entirely. A smile. A big, beautiful, beaming smile. She says, "I did what you said. I swung the bat." I smile back at her and say, "You sure did. You did great. I think you did just great."

Bird's-Eye View

I T WAS AN UNSEASONABLY BEAUTIFUL day in January in East Texas. We'd all been cooped up and bundled up for the last couple of wintery months, and my family was excited to see the first springlike weather of 2015. April was all aflutter around the house, pulling back the curtains, opening windows, and letting fresh air fill the house. It felt amazing, and you could feel the happiness in the air as our daughters ran around and played in the yard, their laughter filling the sky.

There is a window above our kitchen sink that slides open from the side, a window that doesn't have a screen. There is a planter box hanging on the outside that April keeps filled with flowers when the weather turns warm for good. And it's also a popular landing spot for birds. But the happy sounds of the kids playing were just too wonderful to pass up. So even though the occasional bird fluttered by the window, we opened it wide.

I decided it might be a good time to do some writing. I sat down with my laptop and began using this blessed day as an inspiration for some much-needed prose and poetry. After a few minutes, Abby came in the house to get something to drink. She sat down at the dining room table to relax, then suddenly screamed, *"A bird!"* I looked up at her, not fully understanding what she meant. Again she screamed, "A *bird* is in our house! It just flew into your bedroom!" I jumped up from my chair and ran toward the bedroom door. Abby and I both tried to sneak a peek through the door to see if we could spy our feathered intruder. After thoroughly looking around the room from the doorway, I gently stepped inside. I tiptoed around as Abby stood close behind me, nudging me forward. I whispered, "Stop pushing me!" She whispered, "I'm not!" By the way we were acting, you'd think that we were in pursuit of an angry grizzly or something.

We didn't see anything in the bedroom, so I started for the door of our master bathroom. I peeked my head inside, but still no bird. But then I heard it—a small chirp, just a tiny little noise from over near the shower. I still couldn't see him, but I knew he was in there. My wheels started turning. *How can I catch that bird?* First and foremost, I knew I needed to keep him in the bathroom, so I closed the door. I thought that if I used a bedsheet as a net, I could sneak into the bathroom and easily throw the sheet over him (or her, I suppose). Then I would wrap the sheet gently around her/him and carry her/him outside and release her/him to freedom. No problem. Sounds great, doesn't it? Ah, the well-crafted plans of first-time dads.

To begin with, all the sheets were in the bathroom cabinet, and that's where the bird was, in the bathroom. I needed to be able to walk into the room fully prepared, ready for action. April had been doing laundry and, having just learned of our situation, said, "Hey, there's a yellow fitted sheet here in the laundry room." Yes, she said a yellow *fitted* sheet, and as we all know, fitted sheets can ruin the best of days. Fitted sheets aren't user friendly. They're impossible to fold, sometimes even impossible to put on your bed correctly. So I just assumed it would be troublesome while performing the act of bird wrangling as well. But it was all I had.

Well, the sheet didn't hang right. I was holding it up to my side, much like a champion matador approaching his fighting bull from across the pen. I inched closer and closer to the shower, yet I still hadn't seen the bird. Just the occasional chirp let me know we were on the right track. As I came alongside the shower, my fine-feathered friend made his first appearance in our little game of bird and man. With a piercing screech that sounded like a red-tailed hawk, he flew around the corner of the tub at what must've been Mach 3. I don't know, I was kind of winging it there. Could've been Mach 2, I guess. I don't know Machs very well, but it was going really, really fast. And get this, he was brazen enough to dive-bomb my head. Can you imagine?

What happened next comes in small, short memories. I am not certain if I actually suffered a head injury giving me amnesia or if I just sort of blacked out. But here is what I have figured out after some reflection. First, the brazen dive-bomb I mentioned. Then, a very unmanly scream and slap at the bird, which only barely made contact. This slap did, however, upset the bird very much, and he decided to show me just how much he didn't appreciate it. He shifted into supersonic gear (which is beyond Machs) and began angrily circling me, as fast as he could fly, while simultaneously attacking my head. He grabbed my cap, and I swatted him away but at the same time swatted off my cap. This was the first time I really got a glimpse of this flying mammoth. Judging by his massive wingspan, I am not even sure how he got through the window in the first place. Well, he came back for more, and now there was nothing protecting my poor hairless noggin. He had discovered my weakness and was capitalizing on it. His ferocious pterodactyl-like claws made contact with the softness of my scalp, and he was like a lion that has tasted blood. More kamikaze-style flying by the insane bird, and I had yet to have even gotten close to catching the thing. As a matter of fact, I had dropped my *fitted* sheet about halfway through that last dive-bombing. The bird flew over above the tub and paused a minute. I felt sure he was mocking me.

I picked up my *fitted* sheet and headed toward the shower again. This time, he waited. I got closer and closer, and then he dive-bombed my head again, and now he made solid contact with my ear, and I screamed like Daniel Stern in *Home Alone* when that kid puts a tarantula on his face. My fear was now off the charts. On a scale of one to ten, I'd give it a strong twelve.

I eased up to the counter, and he landed behind several cans of April's hair spray, a candle, and a vase, all things that could easily be broken with my spazzy, crazy dad–like movements. But c'mon, this had to be done. I had to catch this bird. Finally, after what must've been three excruciating hours (okay, maybe it was ten minutes) in the torture chamber with this vicious animal, he attempted one last flyby, and I made contact with my cap, which I had grabbed from the floor. The predator finally went down. He wasn't hurt, and he immediately tried to get back up but not before I *fitted* the sheet over him. *Boom!* I dominated the biggest, meanest, most fierce bird that East Texas had ever seen with only my bare hands, a baseball cap, and a fitted bedsheet. Eat your heart out, Bear Grylls.

As I carried the sheet-wrapped bird to the backyard, the girls gathered around to see this wild animal I had conquered. I set the sheet down and began to unfold it. As soon as I pulled the sheet from the top of what surely must be a prehistoric bird that I'd captured, we all stared curiously down at a small brown sparrow. The tiny bird hopped up, shook off his feathers, and flew away, never to be seen again. We stood there speechless until my daughter Emma said, "Was that the right bird? That little ol' bird made you all sweaty like that?"

What? I took a deep breath, grabbed my yellow fitted sheet, and huffed away. Kids seldom realize the lengths we parents go to in order to protect them from, well, sparrows.

The Map to Heaven

APRIL AND I WERE SITTING in the living room, relaxing after a long day. Emma came in carrying her Bible, looking rather studious. She held it up and proudly told us, "This is a map that shows me how to get to heaven." April smiled at our sweet little blue-eyed beauty and said, "Yep, it sure is. That's a great way to think about it. Following what's written in the Bible will lead you right to heaven."

April and I looked at each other and grinned. In that moment we felt really proud. Our girls know that the Bible is the map that gets you to heaven! We must be doing something right! *Good job, Mom and Dad,* we smugly thought to ourselves. Then Emma said,

"No, really, it's the map that gets you to heaven," and then she pointed to the map of Israel that's actually printed in the back of her Bible. Oh, well, yeah, okay. That brought us back down to earth a little bit. I believe *humbled* is the word the Bible uses. Maybe we aren't quite as good at this parenting thing as we thought. But hey, at least she had her Bible out, right? I know, I know, we've got to work on that.

All I Want for Christmas

AH, CHRISTMASTIME. THAT MOST WONDERFUL time of year when we parents spend exorbitant amounts of money on toys, clothes, shoes, boots, coats, hats, and any number of different electronic devices for our children. We do this, you know, to celebrate the birth of our Lord Jesus Christ.

Now, I've gone to church all my life. When I was growing up, my grandpa was our preacher and my grandma was my Sunday school teacher. Although sitting still and listening were not necessarily my strong points, I'm fairly certain I never heard in Sunday school or read in the Bible, "Thou shalt go deep in debt on my birthday." I just don't think that's what the Lord had in mind at Christmas. At the same time, parents enjoy giving gifts to children, seeing their faces light up, hearing their squeals of excitement. And I do believe Jesus enjoys seeing that. So yeah, Christmas can get a little complicated.

April and I were still dating at the time, and I was willing to do anything to make her girls like me. So, with April's help, I bought my first Christmas presents for Abby and Emma. I was so nervous. I wanted so badly to make sure they'd love whatever I got them. I had this vision in my head of those two girls so happy they'd cry and then insist I become their dad on the spot.

But that's not how that Christmas happened. At all. April tells me I have way too high expectations, in everything I do. And I imagine she's right, but I read something when I was a little boy that I've never forgotten. Sam Walton, founder of Walmart, said, "High expectations are the key to everything." I've lived my whole life by that code. I mean, he's Sam Walton. You should probably pay attention to what he has to say. Except maybe when it's in reference to buying your soon-to-be daughters' Christmas presents. In that instance, you should probably keep your expectations pretty darn low. Especially if one of them is Abby, because that girl doesn't get excited about much.

On that Christmas, she opened her gifts, smiled faintly, and then looked away. It's true, we hadn't really established any trust yet, and she was still skeptical of me. But my feelings were crushed. It wasn't her fault. She was just a little girl. Yet it still felt like a straight jab to the kidney. Thanks a lot, Sam Walton.

A ton of water has run under the bridge since then. Abby and Emma have long since accepted me as a dad figure in their lives. Along with the love and comfort we have with each other comes the expectation of the material things a dad should provide for his kids. A few years ago, Abby wouldn't even tell me what she wanted if I begged her. Now, she asks for *everything*. I'm talking EVERYthing. And holy moly, all those things are expensive!

I think back on what Christmas was like for me in the past. Before I had the girls. I pretty much had to get gifts for my mom and dad, and later my nephews, Braden and Joby. A lot of the time, I would simply give my sister money so I could pitch in on whatever she got for them. Christmas wasn't too difficult, nor was it terribly expensive.

Until the last few years, I had never heard of a Lalaloopsy doll, a Flutterbye Fairy, a Monster High doll, or a $115 American Girl doll that needed to get her ears pierced and hair done. (*It's a doll!*) I vaguely knew what Miss Me jeans were, and Ugg boots and Toms shoes, but I for dang sure didn't know how much they cost.

April has always done a great job of providing the girls with the things they want. Still, I like buying the girls things they like and things they will use. Maybe it's that manly need to provide for my family. I don't want to spoil them, but I enjoy the fact that I'm able to give them what they need.

With that being said, when I have spent hard-earned money on something that they "needed" but then never wore it, or never used it, or didn't even know where in the world it was, my brain spirals off into a realm of frustration words cannot describe. Take, for example, Saige, the American Girl doll that we made a special trip to Dallas for, spent the night at the Galleria Mall for, bought a soccer outfit and a horse for, and who now sits in the closet collecting closet dust. Such things make me question my decisions. I know I'm not alone. I mean, they didn't build that gigantic American Girl store only off the money they made from me. That place was packed. I spent $250 total. And there were fifty more poor daddies there at the same time I was, doing the exact same thing. Because we love to make our girls happy. We love that look that says, *Oh, thank you, Dad. I love you.* Even if we spend too much. Then, if only for a moment, it feels like it may have been worth it.

But I'm learning my best bet is not to focus on the amount of money I have spent on clothes, or dolls, or iPads, or iPods, or shoes. Because when I think about the fact that Emma's favorite toys are an old wooden set of crutches that April bought for her for ten dollars at a flea market and a cardboard box from a new toilet I had to install in our guest bathroom, well, I have to revisit some of the focused-breathing techniques we learned in our birthing class right before Gracee was born. And when I go into Abby's closet and find clothes she just had to have that have never been worn and very well may still have the tags on them, then that prescription for antianxiety meds I have sitting in the medicine cabinet suddenly needs to be refilled.

The very reason for this story comes from our friend. Her name is Alexis. She has two kids, and her daughter Katie is Emma's best friend. They are inseparable. Katie spends a lot of time at our house, and Emma spends a lot of time at hers. Katie has a remote-controlled dog, and Emma has been begging us to get her one just like it. There's only one problem: it's a piece of junk. Alexis says it's worthless, and her kids never play with it. Even though it cost seventy-five dollars. It was a complete waste of money. You know what Katie and Emma played with instead of the seventy-five-dollar robot dog? A Walmart sack. They slapped and hit a plastic Walmart sack into the air, over and over, not letting it hit the ground. That was the whole game. *Don't let the bag touch the ground!* They didn't need expensive toys.

They didn't need expensive clothes or shoes or anything else expensive. All they needed was a sack!

With all this new information, my Christmas shopping list just got a whole lot cheaper, and my checking account just got a whole lot fatter. Forget the designer jeans and the fancy toys. Forget the latest iPhone or North Face jacket. We're going to stock them up with grocery sacks and toilet boxes (or other large boxes, if toilet boxes are not available). Because when it comes right down to it, those are the things that seem to be most important to them. And I like that. Because that stuff is cheap. And I like it when things are cheap. Unless it's for me, of course. I don't like cheap stuff.

The Man with All
the Answers

STONEY, WHEN WAS THE POCKET WATCH invented?" I shake my head, being brought back into the present with this random question, one of hundreds I'll undoubtedly be asked this day. I had been daydreaming before I heard the question. I love daydreaming. This time, I was on a hammock, on some remote beach, but there was something peculiar about the scene. First of all, I was alone. That never happens, not anymore. Second, it was quiet. And you're more likely to hit the Powerball than you are to have any silence in my loud group of five.

A long time ago, in a galaxy that feels far away, I was a bachelor.

My home was meticulously cared for, with a place for everything, and everything in its place. Nothing was ever lost, because everything was always where it was supposed to be. But I admit, my favorite part of living alone was the silence. The absence of noise. You know, like quiet moments undisturbed by the sounds of the *Bubble Guppies* or *Doc McStuffins*. Now there's always talking, screaming, crying, tattling, gossiping, laughing, griping. No matter what, there is always something coming out my girls' mouths. And most days, I think I handle it pretty well.

Now, don't get me wrong, I can completely go off the tracks of the crazy train from time to time. But for the most part, I handle their constant buzzing in the background as nothing more than an occasional nuisance. When the girls talk directly to me, they may have to repeat it, because I likely wasn't listening the first time.

When April and I married, Emma was a tiny seven-year-old blonde with sparkling blue eyes and an extremely curious nature. When we first met, she wanted to know everything about me. "Stoney, where are you from?" "Stoney, what kind of truck do you drive?" "Stoney, do you have a nice house? Is it two stories?" "Stoney, do you have a dog?" The questions from this little girl were endless. I immediately loved her for liking me so much, but I truly was not prepared for the number of questions she asked.

The first few times I saw the girls, Emma continued asking one question after another. "Stoney, do you like jalapeños?" "Stoney, why is your house always so clean?" "Stoney, can I play with your guitar?" The stream of questions felt like standing in front of a fire hose with the valve wide open. No mercy.

One of the more memorable questions came after April and I

had been dating awhile. We were on the couch watching TV when Emma dropped this bomb. "Stoney, are you dating anyone other than Mom? Are you gonna be our dad?" Just as calm as she could be, she had just rocked my world. I started to stammer. Now, the correct answer was "No, I'm not dating anyone other than your mother, and oh my gosh, yes, I want to be your dad." But my nerves got soggy, and I hemmed and hawed trying to answer the question while April laughingly watched. Finally, I answered, and while it may not have been the most eloquent answer I've ever given, it was definitely one of the more memorable. And it was the truth. I wanted to be their dad. Oh, and also, I wasn't two-timing their mom.

Time has moved on. We've added another daughter to the mix. We've sure come a long way, but one thing hasn't changed. The questions are just as prevalent today as they ever were. Questions about horses and tennis shoes and go-karts and show pigs, and don't even get me started on the homework questions Emma has about math. I'm convinced those math questions are some kind of punishment on the human race, for what exactly I cannot say.

At this point, I'm willing to bet the questions will never ever end, but I think I'm okay with that. April once asked Emma, "Why do you always ask him questions like that?" Emma replied with full confidence, "Because, Mom, Stoney knows everything." After I heard that, there's never a question I won't answer for her.

Once again, I'm brought back to reality by her question. "When was the pocket watch invented?" With a quick Google search on my phone, I say nonchalantly, "It was invented in 1524." Emma says, "See? He knows everything." Well, maybe with a little help from the internet.

In the time it's taken me to write this, my daughters have each come by and asked me a question. I answered each of them thoroughly, and with a smile on my face. Because I know that someday their mama and I are going to be alone in this house. In a very real sense I'll finally have that quiet I used to crave. And what I expect I'll find is that the silence is just too much. I'm gonna miss all those questions.

The Dirtiest Job of All

I LOVE THE SHOW *Dirty Jobs*. Never mind that I have a minor man crush on Mike Rowe. I think it's really interesting to see all the different dirty, difficult, and odd jobs that people all over the world have. From cleaning septic tanks, to making charcoal, to hauling off dead animal carcasses, he's done pretty much every tough job imaginable, even if for only a day. But there's one job that's left conspicuously off his résumé. He has never been a parent. And I would venture to say that parenting, at least from this dad's perspective, is the dirtiest job there is.

Sure, there are books you can read, videos to watch, and classes you can take, but there's no real way to become qualified, minus having a kid and diving into it headfirst. And while experience is the best teacher, she can be, well, a booger. She has neither mercy, forgiveness, nor compassion, and she has no qualms about letting you fall flat on your face. And even though you don't have to pass a test to become a parent and I felt absolutely unfit for the work, God decided that me having kids would be a good idea. There was no approval certification, no licenses, no graduation ceremony. I was just thrust into parenthood with zero preparation. And I have left a mountain of dirty situations in my wake.

My first massive failure as a parent came years before I actually was one. I went a long time with no children of my own, but my nephews, Braden and Joby, gave me a little experience. They are the sons of my older sister, Shannon, and they are great. I loved playing with them when they were small, but I was admittedly not very careful. I'm big and rough and loud, and I play hard.

One day I somehow convinced my sister to let me take care of them while she went to work at the pharmacy. At the time, they were about seven and nine years old. Our first stop was the Dairy Hut to get some ice cream. Once we were all fully swollen with sugar and energy, we made our way to the local park. We played on the swings for a few minutes, but there was a merry-go-round across the park that was calling my name. It was one of those old heavy steel ones that had sufficient weight to spin you until you puked. They both climbed on. I told them to get a good hold because I was going to give them a wild ride. Braden, the older brother, stood up and held on to one of the pipe handles. Joby, the younger, sat down with one of the pipe handles between his legs, because that was safer, and I was a completely responsible adult, remember?

So once they each had a firm grip, I began to spin. I mean, I really began to spin. Faster and faster and faster, I pushed until the merry-go-round was a blur. The boys were screaming with laughter, and I felt like the greatest uncle in the world. Then all of a sudden, I noticed Joby had closed his eyes and looked a little ashen. I could definitely see some puking in his future. Just when I thought he would surely blow chunks, he lost his grip on the pipe in front of him, his hands flew above his head, and the momentum flung him backward, with his head landing squarely on the rusty head of an old bolt on the floor of the merry-go-round. Immediately I knew I'd made a mistake, but it was far too late. By the time I got the spinning to stop, Joby's head was bleeding in only the way a head wound can—down his forehead and all over his hands. I scooped him off the merry-go-round and began to assess the situation. There was so much blood, I was certain his brains must be hanging out the back of his head. I clamped my hands over where I assumed the massive gash would be. And just like Joby, in short order, I had blood running down my hands and forearms. This was years before Carrie's song, but I was praying, *Jesus, please take the wheel.*

My sister worked at the pharmacy only a few miles away. Joby's bleeding seemed to be subsiding somewhat, so I loaded him into the truck and headed to town. We rushed into the pharmacy looking like something straight out of *Texas Chainsaw Massacre.* Shannon came from behind the counter in a fervor. I felt like I was seven years old again, with my big sister staring me down like a lioness on a wildebeest. My skin felt as though it would melt off my bones as she glared at me. I'd seen this look before. Many times, actually. And usually when she looked at me like that, it was followed by a solid kick to the shins, or maybe the thigh. And it would hurt. However, once she saw all the blood, her face turned white and she had to sit down before she fainted. The bottom line is, I didn't get kicked.

We stuck Joby's head in the bathroom sink and began the process of cleaning it off. We were finally able to see the huge gash on the back of his head. *Wait, what?* That *couldn't* be the cut! It was a tiny little hole. But it was bleeding so much! Well, we finished cleaning Joby up and washed ourselves off so we wouldn't scare the townsfolk as we walked back to the truck. By then some of the color had come back to Shannon's face, which was a huge plus. She even let me leave with her sons once again after we had cleaned Joby's head up. I took them bowling because that was our original plan, but the hole in Joby's noggin had given him a headache and a bit of a sour attitude, so we didn't really have that much fun. To this day, that boy won't get on a merry-go-round. I traumatized him forever. What a mess.

By babysitting my nephews, I had already proven I was in no way qualified to be someone's legal guardian, yet here I am. With three beautiful daughters that I don't understand. And I never will, most likely. Mike Rowe does *Dirty Jobs,* you say? Well, la-di-da. I'm a dad. I've got snot, slobber, burps and farts, smelly feet, random tumbleweeds of hair floating across the floor, and of course the occasional bloody incident from a cut finger or bopped nose.

Dads, moms, parents—we've got the dirtiest job of all. And as for me, I wouldn't trade it for the world. But listen, when it comes to merry-go-rounds, I've hung up my spurs. That was mine, and Joby's, last ride.

Waitin' On a Woman

THE LAST TIME I WAS ON TIME for something? Hmm, let's see, that would've been in August of 2011. You may wonder how in the world I remember that month so clearly, but it's really pretty simple. It's because right after that is when I got married. My days of simply taking a quick five-minute shower, getting dressed in three minutes, and getting out the door in ten were over. I was hypothetically stepping off the high dive into the deep end of the pool. I didn't have a life jacket or an inner tube. I didn't even have any floaties. And let me tell you something, I dang sure didn't know how to swim.

I was drowning. But not in water. I was drowning in women. While most men marry just one woman, I had opted to marry three, sort of. And let me tell you, I didn't have the best track record with even one woman, much less with three at the same time. So to say I was completely out of my element would be a monumental understatement. This dude was lost. Definitely in love, but lost.

My family and friends thought it was hilarious. I had always been this meticulously put-together fellow. My home and truck were clean, and I was never late. Never. To anything. But all that changed when I became a husband and dad. My ten-minute routine fell into a downward spiral I have never recovered from.

Though I'd heard stories from my friends who had daughters, I didn't fully appreciate them until I had daughters of my own. The clothes, the makeup, the hair products, the hair bows, and the nail polish. And the bobby pins, oh my gosh, the bobby pins! Bobby pins are like small magical paper clips that can take a ratty case of bedhead and turn it into a delightful little swept-back look in a matter of moments. *Swept-back look!* I'm pretty proud of myself right now for even knowing what that is. Anyway, the girls had a lot of stuff. And all of it would inevitably end up scattered across the countertops and floors in the bathroom, and maybe even in the sinks and bathtubs. Not to mention the complete jungle of intertwined electric cords for the curling iron, flat iron, and hair dryer. I can guarantee you, it would have taken an entire group of Eagle Scouts to undo that knot.

The first time I knew I was in way over my head was one morning before school. In a desperate attempt to connect with the girls, I offered to take Abby and Emma to school for the first time. How hard could it be? Simple, right? All I had to do was get two girls loaded into the truck, drive to the school, and drop them off. Easy peasy.

No. That was not correct. First, getting them to the truck was similar to herding cats. Especially in the morning. It was mass chaos. Little girls running around with one shoe on, screaming at each other, trying on clothes, then changing clothes and trying on different clothes. Then Abby told Emma, "That doesn't match!" And Emma said, "Yes it does!" And she came running out of her room and stopped right in front of me: "Stoney, Abby says this doesn't match, but it does. Doesn't it?" She was staring at me with those big blue eyes, and I just didn't have the heart to tell her that no, it didn't match. It didn't match at all. But I wouldn't have hurt her feelings for all the gold in California. So I just smiled and said, "Sure, you look great." She smiled a big, smug smile and said, "Told you, Abby!" Abby was eleven years old and at the time hadn't decided if she liked me yet. In fact, she was determined not to like me. With a roll of her eyes and a sideways glance, she said, "He's just a guy. He doesn't know if you match or not."

With that little jab, I said, "Okay, girls, we're running late. We've got to go!" We rushed out the door and headed for my truck. Abby never uttered another word to me, and Emma didn't stop talking all the way to school. I dropped Abby off right as the bell was ringing, but Emma was a few minutes late. Right then and there, my immaculate record of promptness came to an end. I called April and told her, a tad disappointed in myself. She laughed and said, "Don't worry about it. It won't be the last time." Boy, how true that statement turned out to be.

Being on time is now some distant memory of a faraway time. Abby is eighteen now, Emma is fourteen, and Gracee is five. And of course, there's April. With the four of them, things that were once so simple, like going out to dinner, are now much more complicated endeavors. Even the most casual settings call for a fresh change of clothes, makeup, fixing hair, and most likely, changing clothes. There's always the potential for screaming, the possibility of crying, and the probability of one heck of a big pile of laundry. Usually one of them, if not all four, can't find their shoes. But over time I guess I've mellowed a bit. These days, instead of getting too stressed out about it, I just laugh as I watch them run through the house.

Nowadays, when Emma asks, "Stoney, do I match?" I tell her the truth. "No, honey. You don't match at all." But she doesn't really care because she's going to wear it anyway. Because I'm just a guy. And guys don't know if you match or not. At least that's what Abby said, and I've learned a thing or two from her. And I'm still learning.

People Germs

I WAS BORN AND RAISED on a large quarter-horse ranch in northeastern Oklahoma. Getting dirty was just a given. Fixing fences, cleaning stalls, doctoring horses and cattle—it was all just a part of a normal day. I went to college on an equine scholarship, where, among other things, I became a certified AI technician, which means that on any given day, you could find me shoulder deep in the nether regions of a cow, horse, or pig. No, AI does not stand for "artificial intelligence."

I can do all those things and never bat an eye. I guess because they seem part of my DNA, I don't even hesitate. Getting dirty while working the land or handling my farm animals doesn't bother me one bit. But here's the kicker. People germs? They make me want to bathe in acid. I do not like touching people. Adults, kids, doesn't matter. I hate it. And public bathrooms? Good grief, don't even get me started.

Case in point. I recently had to use a gas station restroom. I drive a lot for my job. And drink loads of coffee. Yes, do the math. I found a station that looked clean enough, and since I was about to pee my pants, I decided to give it a try. Mistake. This bathroom only had an electric hand dryer in it. Not an automatic hand dryer, mind you, but one with a button you have to push. I did not want to touch that button. It looked filthy, and wet. However, I couldn't leave my hands wet, nor could I use toilet paper to dry my hands. You're probably wondering why not, right? Well, I would have felt even more disgusted touching toilet paper that had been sitting in the dirty bathroom than touching the button on that hand dryer. I know, weird. But that's me.

So I washed my hands and pushed the nasty button with my arm so I could dry them. But when I touched the button with my arm, it felt totally gross and skanky, so I then felt the overwhelming need to wash my hands, and arm, again. Back at the sink, I washed to the elbows like I was getting ready to perform an actual emergency appendectomy. But of course, I was still in the predicament of how to turn on the hand dryer. This time, I tried to use my cloth-covered shoulder, but there was a problem. This button was one that you just touch, and it uses the body heat from your hand, or some such sorcery, to turn it on. And my clothed shoulder didn't have the magic.

Reluctantly, I tried to use my elbow, and it worked. The dryer came on. And I felt fairly certain that if I were to hold my wet hands in front of my face, and blow as hard as I could with my own mouth and lungs, I could've dried my hands more quickly. Also, when the dryer started blowing, it put out a horrible, sulfuric smell, which made my hands feel dirty all over again. I knew I had to get out of that bathroom. I turned to leave, and *of course* the door had a knob, and it had to be pulled open and not kicked open like a SWAT team would, which is exactly what I felt like doing.

I untucked my shirt so I could use my shirttail to grab the doorknob and open the door. Just as I twisted the knob and unlocked it, a dude from the outside hit the door like a Spanish fighting bull, and the doorknob touched my bare belly. And the door *touched my cheek*. IT. TOUCHED. MY. CHEEK. Shock. Horror. Mayhem. Pandemonium, and whatnot. I rushed as quickly as I could from the restroom to my truck. It was time for total damage control. I bathed myself in antibacterial gel. My hands, arms, and face. And stomach. It burned my eyes and a cut on my hand, so I knew it was working. Then I drove straight across town about fifteen minutes to this big, nice gas station that I *knew* had nice, clean bathrooms, with the zigzag entrances, automatic faucets, and Dyson Airblade hand dryers. And I washed my hands. Ooh, I washed my hands. And it was glorious.

Unfortunately, this is just one example of the countless stories in my life that end eerily similar to this one. My germaphobic ways were completely manageable when I lived all by my lonesome. I could line my boots up under the stairs just the way I wanted. I could vacuum every night without fear of disturbing someone or waking them up. I could wash my one plate, my one fork, and my one glass, and put them right back into my cabinet. My world was a neatly folded, perfectly kept environment (and lonely).

For someone as particular and completely anal-retentive as I am, moving three women into my house was about the most traumatic thing that could have happened. I can only imagine how unbearable I was to live with those first few months. My neat little world had been turned upside down, and I had no idea how to handle it.

Where I had once found clean countertops, I now found spilled Kool-Aid, bobby pins, and strands of hair. Where I had once seen shiny and clean bathroom floors, I now found an unimaginable pile of little girls' pants and underwear and socks and towels. Where there had once been a clean kitchen sink, there was now a plate filled with food, just left there. The things I have seen, the messes I have cleaned up, the chaos that is raising children, was something that I could never have planned for. But as God knew and I'm learning, it was exactly what I needed.

Now, don't get me wrong, I still lose my mind from time to time. I still use antibacterial gel like it's going out of style. I wash my hands every thirty minutes, all day long, often until my knuckles are raw. I still lock the front and back doors three times before going to bed. I still tap my toes three times into the bottom of my boots before putting them on. Because hey, I'm still me, and I'm still a little odd. Actually, I'm a lot odd. Now if you'll excuse me, it's time to go wash my hands.

Dad Talk

I LOVE BEING A DAD. I REALLY DO. That's a super hilarious thing to hear myself say. And I'm sure anyone who has known me for any amount of time thinks it's even funnier than I do. But I do, I love being a dad.

For years I swore I'd never have kids. I was certain of it. It just wasn't the direction I imagined my life would ever take. My friends were parents, also my sister, my cousins. I watched them interact with their children. I saw them doting and swooning over every little thing. Every silly smile, raised eyebrow, burp, or giggle would bring about a round of applause not unlike what you might expect to hear during the encore of a Led Zeppelin concert. The adoring oohs and aahs and laughter of the approving parents were sweet, for a minute. Sure, they were proud. Sure, they thought their kid was the cutest kid on the planet. And the smartest. And the most athletic. I guess that's just human nature.

I just didn't understand this behavior. Sure, they were cute kids. I would briefly play with them or aggravate them. I liked to make them laugh. But the first hint of a cry, or a snotty nose, or a poopy diaper, and this boy was out. I wanted nothing to do with it. I have a horrible confession to make. Don't think badly of me, okay? When people look at newborn babies and say things like "Oh, he's so cute; he looks just like his daddy!" or "Oh my goodness, she's so precious; she looks just like her mama!" or "She's got her daddy's nose" or "Look at that little dimple when she smiles. Just like her papa!" Okay, seriously. I don't see any of that. I try, I really do. I look at them, and I grin and nod my head. But I don't see anything like that. All I see is a little squashed-up face with wrinkly skin and a bald head with no teeth. I suppose they look more like my ninety-year-old granddad than anything. But I can't really say that unless I want to be disowned and banished by pretty much everyone.

There were few things I was certain of in life, but I was sure I'd never become one of those embarrassingly proud daddies who gloated over a child's every move. Or so I thought.

Fast-forward a few years. April came along, with her two beautiful daughters. I took the whole mess of them under my wing, and I never looked back. All of a sudden I was a dad. It all happened so fast, I couldn't believe it. I found myself in laughable situations that were unfathomable only a short time before.

Suddenly, I was at the American Girl store, surrounded by thousands of dolls and giddy, squealing little girls. Several hundred bucks later, I found myself outside on the sidewalk wondering what had just happened. I found myself on the sidelines at a peewee football game, cheering on my own adorable little cheerleader, just praying that today would finally be the day she won the spirit stick. I found myself taking them to haunted houses, to the mall, and to little-kid movies. But it didn't stop there. Oh, no.

I believe being a parent brings out the best in people. It makes you want to be better. It brings out a whole other side you didn't even know existed. And yes, it brings out the completely goofy. You know exactly what I mean, don't you? Because your kids make you act goofy too. It's okay, you can admit it. It brings out the goofiest in all of us. Think about it. Think about holding your little baby above your head, looking at his or her smiling, toothless face. What would you do? What would you say? I'll tell you what you would say. You would say, "Shmoopy-poopy-dooboo! I wuv you, wittle baby doll! You're such a beautiful wittle baby booboo!" Or something very similar to that. I guarantee it.

Here is a prime example of just how goofy my own child can make me and of the silly things I say that I never dreamed would escape my lips. The other day we went to our friends' house for their daughter's second-birthday party. There were little girls everywhere. Dolls, balloons, cupcakes, and toys all over the place, as is usual for a second-birthday party. Or so I would assume. I guess this was actually the first time I'd ever attended a second-birthday party.

Anyhow, the girls and their mothers stayed out on the patio, went swimming, and played around in the yard while the dads sat inside and watched the Sooners / Tulsa Golden Hurricanes game.

We talked about football; we talked about teams' defenses, their offenses, overrated teams, underrated teams, and who we thought would end up in the playoffs this year. You know—man stuff.

As we sat there talking about all of those "manly" things, our daughters would enter the room for a few minutes, only to turn and run back out again. It wasn't until the night was over that I began to think about some of the things we'd said when our daughters burst into the room. Our conversations were borderline ridiculous. Here is an excerpt from our football-watching/man-talking/daddy-daughter conversations:

Man 1 (to his daughter): Honey, do you need to go pee pee? Do you need to pee pee? Let's go pee pee.

Man 1 (to us): We're going to start potty training soon. INTERCEPTION! Did you see that? Great play!

Man 2 (to his wife): Hey, Mom, do you know where Hadley's LuLu is? She really needs her LuLu and her bop-bop, and then I'll put her down for a wittle nap.

Man 2 (to us): GO DEEP! Did you see that sick block? He totally laid him out!

Man 3 (that's me): No, no, Gracee. No. You need to sit on your bottom or you'll fall and hurt yourself. Thank you; that's a good girl. Oh, those are sweet kisses! Smoochy smoochy smooch smoochy! (And then I swooped her up in my arms and kissed and nibbled and blew zerberts on her neck while she giggled the cutest giggle that has ever been giggled.)

Man 4 (to everyone): Hey, does anyone know where her
    Binky is? We've got to find it, seriously. We don't find it,
    then stuff is about to get real. No, she doesn't like that one,
    the nipple is too small. We've got to find the other one.
    TOUCHDOWN! I think it was a really good move
    putting Blake Bell over into the tight-end slot. You know
    he's going to pick up three or four yards on every play.

So apparently this is just how we talk now. Pee pees and Binkies
and LuLus mixed in with football and the occasional cussword. Dad
talk. It's a real thing. If you're a young dude out there reading this
right now and you're thinking, *This is all just so silly. That will never
be me. No way. Not a chance,* then I say—you wanna bet? Yes. Yes,
it will. You will be powerless over it. Don't feel bad, though. It's taken
down the best of us. But guess what else? You're going to love it like
nothing you've ever known. I'll bet on it.

Don't Tease the Llamas

S o, in the summer of 2012, the girls had finally gotten moved down from Oklahoma, once school was out. It was a fairly traumatic thing, moving them away from their home, their school, and their friends and family. Not just for Abby and Emma, either. April had quite a bit of adjusting to do as well.

To try to make the move as easy as possible, I was pretty much willing to do anything or go anywhere if I thought they might enjoy it. So when I saw the sign for Cherokee Trace Drive-Thru Safari, I knew immediately it would be a pick-me-up, that it was something all my animal-loving girls would enjoy.

So one hot, muggy Saturday afternoon, we made the thirty-mile drive south of Tyler to this drive-through zoo. I've been to one of these before but not since I was a little kid. Frankly, there were a few traumatizing events that happened back then, so I'm not sure what it was that made me think this time would be any different.

But I was so happy that the girls were finally with me in Texas, and I wanted to see them laugh, smile, and be happy. So we checked in at the office, I paid our entry fee, I bought us each a bag of food, and we made our merry way into the happy land of goats, deer, deer, goats, a few cows, some ill-tempered Sicilian donkeys, goats, deer, buffalo, and maybe a few pigs. And some goats and deer. Seriously, it was mostly goats and deer. I promise.

However (pause for dramatic effect), there were also some llamas. This changed the entire tone of our time together because I believe that llamas are stupid, sorry, no-count jerks. I realize that sounds very judgmental, but I don't like llamas. I just don't.

As we approached the "llama area" in my brand-new truck (did I mention my *brand-new* truck?), three animals quickly perked up, looked in our direction, and came hurriedly toward us at a high lope. The girls oohed and aahed over the cute little llamas. "Oh, look at them!" "They are so cute!" "Look at their ears; they're so big!" "Look how long their eyelashes are!" "Oh, I'm gonna feed them!"

I have always been pretty good at doing funny voices, so I began to talk in a voice I felt a llama would use, just saying silly things that would make the girls laugh. And man, were they *laughing*. I felt great! They seemed to be having such a fun time! They seemed to be so happy! Way to go, Stone!

As the girls began to feed them, it was easy to see there was definitely an alpha among the three, and as is often the way with alphas, he was kind of a jerk. He made a funny hissing noise the girls thought was "so cute!" He pinned his ears back and would stick his head through the window to get the food. Having been around horses all my life, I can tell a surly animal when I see one. And he definitely was. I told them to be careful. I told them he was about to get ignorant. But no, no one listens to me. I'm just their chauffeur and arm candy.

When he came around to my side of the truck, I rolled my window up, because I'm smart. Even with being heckled by all the females in my *brand-new* truck, I would not roll it down. I said, "Girls, that llama's not playing! I'm telling you, he's getting ready to throw a fit!" To which April replied, "Oh, quit being such a *baby*!" My lovely wife would pay for this silly remark. Unfortunately, we would all have to pay for it.

Alpha llama began to butt his head against my closed window, yet still no one heeded my warnings. He went around to April's side and hissed. So as you might expect, she gave him some food. He took it and hissed again. I said, "April, darling, I am begging you, please roll up your window!" To which she replied, "He's just playing, Stoney!"

As soon as April said "just playing," alpha llama unleashed the most disgusting combination of bodily functions and bodily fluids that have ever been combined on this earth. It was a massive conglomeration of a gassy, belching cough that was filled with slimy green whatever-is-inside-a-llama. I know that's gross, but that's what blew in my *brand-new* truck. Then, to top it all off, alpha llama let out a hair-raising scream at the end. All of this, no more than three inches from April's face.

In an instant, we went from laughing and having a blast to experiencing one of the worst days of our new lives together. That horribly gross green stuff I mentioned in the last paragraph? Yeah, it was all over the inside of my windshield, all over my dash, and it covered my rearview mirror to the point that I couldn't see anything in it. My GPS screen, yep, covered. Steering wheel, check. Sun visors, check. My plaid khaki golf shorts? Slimed. I could feel it on my face, my neck, my ears. Everywhere. You may recall I'm a germaphobe.

All this time, April had her hands over her face. The girls were in the back seat, laughing as if they had just witnessed something from *America's Funniest Home Videos*. April uncovered her face, and I couldn't really get a grasp of her emotions. I think she definitely wanted to cry. But I also had the feeling she thought it was pretty funny, even as the gross green stuff dripped from her hair.

But our main problem was we couldn't get out of the truck because to step outside my no-longer-brand-new truck would mean facing the llamas. So I did what any levelheaded person with slime in his ears would do—I hit the gas and drove away. But guess who started following us? That's right. The faster I drove, the faster they ran. We bounced around the cab as I drove forty miles per hour across a pasture. Old Mac Davis thought happiness was Lubbock, Texas, in his rearview mirror. I knew for a fact that happiness was llama land in mine.

At some point we finally lost the llamas. I hit the brakes, and we bailed out of the truck while simultaneously trying to wipe the foul mess off our bodies. I don't think I've ever felt so dirty. It was awful. Plus, my *brand-new* truck . . . I'm sorry, I get all choked up just thinking about it.

We gathered our wits about us (girls still laughing) and headed for home. As we were leaving, we noticed another car pulling into the llama area. We watched as those stupid, sorry, good-for-nothing llamas moved in to take advantage of another unsuspecting family. And I think we laughed all the way home.

I had prayed for a fun, memorable day, one the girls would never forget. Moral of the story? God answers prayers, so be careful what you ask for.

Just Let It Happen

ONE DEFINITION OF *vacation* is "a specific trip, usually for relaxation, recreation, and tourism." The key word there for most people would be *relaxation*. Prior to five years ago, taking a vacation was about the last thing on my mind. I worked, I played golf, I played guitar in the evenings, and I went to bed. That was pretty much my life. But then when April and I got together and I was suddenly the father to her two daughters, I soon realized that vacation was a regular part of family life, one that was looked forward to all year long, something that involved planning and savvy financial maneuvering. I was constantly reminded by all three of my lovely ladies: "Where are we going this year?" "Are we going to Destin again?" "Can we go snorkeling?" "Can we rent a boat and go to

Crab Island?" "Can we go parasailing?" The list of "can we's" seems to be never ending. And the opposite of cheap.

For the family accountant (me), the *relaxation* becomes more difficult as vacation looms. The cost of renting a beach house, gas, flights, rental cars, and daily expeditions can be daunting. Then there's the food. And the price tag just keeps getting higher and higher. Yes, I know there are less expensive ways to go to the beach, but these are memories we are making, right? I like being able to give my family things they enjoy. So even though staying in the Motel 6 is tempting, I generally bend to their wishes. This year was no exception. We got a beautiful condo right on the beach in Destin, Florida. We would leave during the last week of June and stay through the Fourth of July weekend.

I love my family. But not a one of them are angels, and that includes me. Put five normal, human, nonangelic beings in a vehicle for the ten-and-a-half-hour drive from East Texas to the Emerald Coast of Florida and chances are good every emotion on the spectrum will be covered. In other words, our trip usually contains "all the feels." Is there any way to remedy that? There might be, but let me tell you what I did that year. I invited two more people.

Yes, you read that right. We invited two more people to go on vacation with us—April Hicks and her daughter Maggie. My wife and April have been best friends since the sixth grade. So our departing total was six women and girls. And me. In one car. In one condo. For a whole week. I was equal parts excited and terrified. But I can explain.

April and Maggie are our dear friends, and they had just recently suffered a terrible loss. Only five weeks prior to our vacation, April's husband, Todd, passed away after an awe-inspiring battle against ALS. For five years, he fought this disease for which there is no cure, knowing full well what his fate would someday be. Yet he and April courageously soldiered to the end.

April and I thought that taking them on vacation with us, away from the worries and stresses they'd endured for the last several years, would be a great start to get them back on track. So they drove to Texas from Oklahoma, and the next morning, bright and early, all seven of us headed to Destin.

I felt like Todd was watching over us—and laughing—as the car pulled away filled to the brim with his wife and daughter and my wife and daughters. Only a fool would make such a trip this out-numbered. Alas, I am a fool. We left early in the morning so the girls could go back to sleep and sleep through the first three or four hours of the trip, and it worked! They all slept until we were nearly in Mississippi, and then they listened to music and watched movies on their iPads. They laughed and they looked at the battleships in Mobile Bay and watched for dolphins at Pensacola Beach. They didn't fight or cry or scream. They were amazing. It was the most problem-free, stress-free cross-country trip any of us could have ever dreamed of. It was almost too good to be true. The two Aprils and I were ecstatic.

As we pulled into the driveway of our condo, the kids were al-ready getting antsy to get to the beach. So we let them get their swimsuits on, and they all went down to the beach while I unloaded the car. Once it was unloaded, I put on my swim trunks and joined them. We played for a few hours, then dressed for dinner. I then had the best plate of oysters I've ever shoved into my piehole. I didn't want to get ahead of myself, but if the rest of this vacation went like the first day, this was going to be the greatest week anyone has ever had. And it turned out to be just that, a great week for everyone.

Near the end of our week together, the two wives and I were sitting and talking on the beach. April H. said, "What do I do? I am a thirty-five-year-old widow. How do I go on without him?" Tears started flowing from both of them. Then she said, "And what about Maggie? How do I raise her alone? She needs a daddy! I'm just so scared." I started to give her the same old cliché things that everyone always says when something bad happens: "You'll be fine." "You are strong." "You just need time to heal." But those words felt so weak and empty. So we simply gave her a hug and wiped away our tears. I stood up and headed out into the water with the kids, who were busy fighting waves.

A few minutes later, the women came out to where we were playing. April H. is not very tall, and the waves that day were big. A few of them crashed in over her head. My daughter Emma was laughing and said to her, "April, sometimes when those great big waves come in, I just close my eyes, grit my teeth, and let it happen. They knock me down, but I just get back up again."

April and I looked at each other and smiled. In that instant, the words we had struggled to find to console and encourage April H. in her time of need had just inadvertently rolled off the tongue of our spirited and innocent little blonde. I said, "There's your words of wisdom." Life can be full of big waves and rocky seas. Sometimes they knock you down. But you just have to keep getting up.

Pineapple

AYING "I LOVE YOU" is not always the easiest thing to do, especially when you have a new stepdaughter and she's a bit of a cautious type anyway. I didn't want to be pushy, but I really wanted to tell her, and I thought she wanted to tell me too, but it just felt sort of awkward. We needed some way to say "I love you" without saying it, if that makes any sense. Well, it did to us, so Abby and I came up with a code word to use in its place—*pineapple*. Yes, I'm serious. It was more comfortable for both of us in the beginning, but I admit that now, in my relationship with Abby, I actually prefer *pineapple* to the actual sentence.

It's ours, and only ours, and I love it. It makes me happy, every time I hear it. "I love you" is heard by countless people every day. But how many people hear the word *pineapple* and feel loved?

Silence Is Golden

ENJOY BEING ALONE. I DO. I love silence. I can go hours at a time without speaking to anyone, without any type of human interaction at all. Now, this revelation makes me quite a ball of complexities, I will admit, because anyone who knows me knows I can talk as much as anyone you have ever met. Put me in a crowd or at a party, and watch the stories begin to flow out of me like Niagara Falls. As a matter of fact, my talkativeness as a child is still fodder for conversations at many of our family gatherings. By most accounts, the only time I wasn't talking was when I was asleep. And I didn't sleep very much. And not only do I talk a lot, but I also have a very loud, deep, boisterous voice that can be heard from a mile away. Being sneaky has never been a strong suit of mine. So I suppose it is odd for someone like me to cherish silence and serenity as much as I do.

But here's the deal. I'm a dad. I'm a family man, and my family needs me. At any given time, I am needed by one or all of them, and the things they need from me are countless. Now, don't get me wrong. I love my role as dad and husband. I am the provider and protector of my family, and that is not a responsibility I take lightly. However, every once in a while, I confess a little break wouldn't be bad. Does that make me a bad parent? I sure hope not. I love these girls more than life itself, but geez louise, they can work a man to death and ask questions until the cows come home.

Case in point, I got home one night recently after a long day at work. It was already dark outside as I walked in the door and set my briefcase on the floor, ready to grab a drink and sit in my recliner. But oh, no. My girls had other plans. First, Gracee saw me. "Dad!" she yelled and ran to me with arms wide open. With complete trust, she leaped into the air, knowing I would catch her. And just as she knew I would, I caught her under her arms and pulled her up to my face. She smelled clean, and her hair was wet from the bath. I kissed her soft cheeks and neck with a fervor that always makes her giggle. Unfortunately, it also makes her squirm and kick her feet, and there is only one place those little feet will make contact with my body, and it is the one place a man never wants to get kicked. Just like clockwork, her little foot of fury connected solidly between my legs. I groaned and set her down. "Sorry, Dad!" she yelled over her shoulder as she quickly ran into her bedroom to play. With my hands on my knees, trying to catch my breath and get this sick feeling out of my gut, I heard the other two daughters come sauntering up to me. I asked them about their day and got the exact answer I expected: "Fine." About that time April walked up and gave me a kiss and asked me about my day. All in all, it was a warm, welcoming homecoming. The best part of my day, without a doubt.

And then, it began. Emma came walking up to me with algebra homework in her hands and a look of frustration on her face. "Stoney, I have no idea how to do these problems. I don't know how to do these! I'm going to fail!" We sat down at the kitchen table and began to go over the list of equations that had Emma nearly in tears. After fifteen minutes or so of arguing, fighting, crying, and laughing, we finally found the right answer for the first problem. She finally understood. But before the ink was even dry on that algebra nightmare, Abby was standing next to me. "Stoney, we've got to have my speech presentation completed and turned in by Saturday! We haven't even started!" I replied, "Wait, wait, wait. *You've* got to get the presentation done by Saturday, not me." "But, Stoney! I need your help! Can we please sit down and start writing it tonight?" "Okay, give me a minute." We spent the next hour discussing the topic of the upcoming speech she will be presenting at the Houston Livestock Show and Rodeo. We came up with a good plan, and I am pleased with what she will present.

I felt the tiredness beginning to drag down on me, in my shoulders and neck. I was ready to relax. Just then I heard, "Dad! I need you to read me a book before I go to bed!" Now, you may think that reading a three-year-old a bedtime story would be an easy task, but you don't know what kind of kid we are dealing with. If you'll refer back to the first paragraph, you'll see where I say I was a loud kid who never stopped talking. Well, Gracee is a carbon copy of me. Reading her a book is a marathon of reading and intermittently having her own stories thrown in there for you to listen to. So I read for a bit; then she talked for a bit. We did that song and dance until, finally, I had to put my boot down. "No, ma'am. No more. It's time for bed." After a few tears, she snuggled into her bed, and I headed back to the living room. My recliner was in sight, and I could not wait to get into it. I sat down, closed my eyes, let out a long exhale, releasing all of the stress from my day. Ah yes, there it is. The silence I've been waiting for all day. Sweet, beautiful silen—

"Dad!"

Well, I guess there's always tomorrow.

Don't Blink

I SQUEEZED ABBY TIGHT. She's normally not much of a hugger, but this day, I just didn't care. I held her for a bit too long because I just wasn't ready to let go. She hugged me back but said, "Oh my gosh, stop! It's no big deal."

But it was a big deal. It was her last first day of school, the first day of her senior year of high school. She hadn't gotten her driver's license by the first day of her junior year, so this was also the first time we had not driven her to school on the first day. In other words, she was driving herself.

So standing there in the driveway, I held that hug as long and as tight as I could, gave her a quick kiss on the cheek, and finally let her go. Her mom then stepped in, with big tears in her eyes, and Abby understood that another big hug was imminent. April wrapped her up in her arms, and Abby's awkwardness sort of fell away, and she melted into her mother's arms. They stood there in silence for a few moments, a beautiful mother/daughter moment that's indicative of the amazing bond they have with each other.

April was nineteen years old when she had Abby, so not only are they mother and daughter, but they're also best friends. April let go of her and looked her in the eyes. She said, "You're going to do great. It's your last year of being a kid, so enjoy it." Then I opened her car door for her and helped her into her car, even though she thought I was acting silly.

As her mother and I watched her drive away, I felt a tear roll down my cheek. I quickly wiped it away, hoping April didn't see it, but she did. I felt her arm slide around my waist as she said, "You're such a big softie." And she's right. I am.

It used to get on my nerves when people would say things like "Don't blink. Next thing you know, they'll be all grown up" or "They just grow up so fast. You'd better enjoy it while you can." It always felt like such a downer thing to say to someone who was enjoying living in the moment, taking our kids to softball games and livestock shows and cheerleading at football games. I didn't want to be told about how quickly it would be gone. Just let me enjoy it! Let me have my happy moment with my daughters without having to think about what it's going to be like when they're gone.

I taught Emma to tie her shoes when she was seven. She weighed probably forty-five pounds. I set her little body on my lap, and we tied them and untied them over and over again. And then one day, finally, it clicked. We celebrated and laughed and high-fived. It was such a small thing, but for as long as I live, I'll never forget that moment.

Now I look at her, and she's beautiful and thirteen years old. She shaves her legs and gets BO and wears the same size shoe as her mother. That tiny little girl is gone, just a sweet memory, although for the most part, she is still every bit as entertaining as she ever was.

Abby, on the other hand, was older and more cautious with me when I first came around. She was more closed off, and it took me a while to gain her trust. But very few seventh graders don't need help with math homework. And I'm pretty good at math, so that worked out in my favor. I'd spend those few minutes each night helping her with her homework. Slowly but surely, she came around. We got closer each and every day until, eventually, we couldn't have been closer. She grew up from that little chubby-cheeked preteen girl into the beautiful brunette young woman I am now helping into her car, on her last first day of school.

We watched her pull out of the driveway and then drive away, and we began walking back to the house. April squeezed my hand and said with a tremble in her voice, "I just can't believe it. It seems like just yesterday that I dropped her off at preschool. She should still be my little girl, sitting in my lap reading bedtime stories." I squeezed her hand back and said, "Yeah, I know. It's like we just blinked."

Dressing Girls Is Hard

SUMMERTIME MEANS VERY DIFFERENT things to parents than it does to children, doesn't it? For the children, it just means No School. But for the parents, it means the kids are going to be home *all the time*. And for us, that's especially true, because we don't have any family nearby, so they are home ALL THE TIME.

So, as our children see their three months of freedom coming to an end, we see nine months of freedom just beyond the horizon, waiting for us. Yes! Hallelujah!

When Emma was in the third grade, April and I hadn't even been married a year. So having only been a dad to her two daughters since that time, there were certain things that continued to baffle me daily, school or no school. I had to become accustomed to the daily comings and goings of the prepubescent female. And without a doubt, one of the most difficult and sometimes infuriating things I had ever had to do in my life was the simple act of getting girls ready for school and out the door. To say it was quite an educational experience is an understatement of epic proportions. It's like calling a slice of crispy, fried, delicious bacon just a piece of meat. It's much, much more than that. There have been many, many things I have learned.

One of those many things that have left me scratching my head, day in and day out, has been getting our daughter Emma dressed in a respectable and presentable manner, on my own. She is without a doubt the most flamboyant and eccentric individual I've ever known. No amount of sparkle is enough. She wants loud, flashy colors, sparkly shoes, rhinestone belts, bright red lipstick, shiny, gaudy jewelry, and as much pomp and circumstance as humanly possible. Nothing is too ostentatious. Nothing is too over the top. Admittedly, her spunky attitude and extravagant taste in clothing and accessories can be completely adorable. But if you are a new dad, just trying to get by, it can be unbelievably exasperating.

As April became more and more pregnant by the day with our youngest daughter, Gracee, and sleeping less and less, I tried to give her all the time to rest that I could. So I took on the responsibility of getting the girls up and dressed and then delivered them to school before I left for work every day. Waking them up? No problem. Getting them some breakfast? Easy. Getting Emma dressed in clothes that wouldn't embarrass her mother to the point of not wanting to go out in public? Not quite so simple. If left to her own devices, Emma could easily go to school looking like Cyndi Lauper and Boy George had a secret love child and then hired George Clinton to be her stylist. It's gonna be funky and cool. Trust me.

One sunny day in March, tragedy struck. Now, I had definitely let her get to school in some questionable outfits before. The occasional raised eyebrows from April when we got home were a telltale sign of disapproval. Generally, in the mornings, I was more concerned with getting them out the door and to the school before the bell rang. So she may have flown under the radar a few times in Moon Boots and a tutu. But on this day, I'll admit, it's possible I simply wasn't paying attention. I was talking on the phone as she came out a minute or so after Abby and climbed into the back seat. Off to school we go. "Bye, girls! Have a great day!" I said. And then I headed to work.

Well, that morning, April began to have a few contractions, and I was afraid to get too far from home, so I worked from home that afternoon. Around three o'clock, April and I went to get the girls from school. First we picked up Abby and then headed to the elementary school to get Emma. We pulled up, and as Emma walked up to the truck, my world began to change. She was wearing a yellow shirt. So far, so good, right? Red hair bow. Okay, probably not the best choice, but we'll take it. There were sparkly pink-and-silver Toms on her feet. Yeah, it's getting worse. However, on bottom, she was wearing a pair of old faded-yellow dollar-store pajama pants with green writing on them that were much too short, coming only just below her knees. But then there were black tights protruding beneath the pajama pants. The poor girl looked like a tiny hobo.

As her teacher walked her up to the car, April wheeled around on me like a mama bear: "*What* did you send her to school in?" I stumbled and stuttered for an answer, but I simply didn't have one. "April, I swear I've never seen those pants in my life. That's not what she was wearing when I dropped her off this morning!" As Emma got in the truck, April turned to the back seat. "Emma, what in the world are you wearing?" Emma rolled her eyes and said, "Well, Mom, I was bent over my desk signing my homework, and Mrs. Elliott came running up to me and said, 'Emma, you can't wear those pants because I can see through them.' And then she sent me to the nurse's station, and they told me I had to put these stupid pajama pants on because I was only wearing pantyhose! And these pants are the ones they give to the kids who pee their pants at school. But I'm pretty sure they're clean."

April spun back around. "You sent her to school in pantyhose?" My mouth opened and I tried to speak, but no words came out. In my defense, the sun hadn't been all the way up yet, and I couldn't see her all that well. And where the heck was my backup? Abby was supposed to watch me and make sure I didn't do something stupid! She totally let me down.

Well, I learned an important lesson that day. Pantyhose, and only pantyhose by themselves, are extremely inappropriate attire for school. Or, really, for anything. At all. Anywhere. Well, now I know. Next time she tries that with me, I'll be all over it. I'll say, "No way, José. It ain't happenin'."

Yeah, next time. Like a boss.

Never Let You Down

I HAVE ALWAYS ENJOYED WRITING poems, songs, and short stories. Most of them never see the light of day, but this one, well, this one's different. I hope you enjoy it.

She sits staring out the window
Watching for his truck to pull in the drive
He said he'd be here at three thirty
But now it's fifteen after five

Her sister sits in her bedroom
'Cause she knows that he won't show

Too many times left disappointed
She quit believing long ago

A girl needs a daddy
And he's just never been
He hasn't done what he said he'd do
Since I can't remember when
But I'll be right here waiting
So that when you come around
I'll do everything a dad should do
And I'll never let you down

Years have passed. He still ain't here
So I'm your ride to the mall
I see you staring at your phone
To see if you missed his call
You tell me "Thanks" and hop on out
I'll just come back to pick you up
I whisper "I love you" under my breath
As you walk away from my truck

A girl needs a daddy
And he's just never been
He hasn't done what he said he'd do
Since I can't remember when
But I'll be right here waiting
So that when you come around

Never Let You Down

I'll do everything a dad should do
And I'll never let you down

The preacher says, "Who gives this woman?"
My voice trembles, "Her mother and I"
Next to me, your mother is sniffling
And you're there all dressed in white
You kiss my cheek and tell me, "Thank you"
And you whisper to me, "Don't be sad"
I grit my teeth, fight back tears, and say,
"Thanks for letting me be your dad"

A girl needs a daddy
And he'd just never been
He hadn't done what he said he'd do
Since I can't remember when
But I was right there waiting
And when you finally came around
I did everything I knew to do
I hope I didn't let you down

We Bought a Farm

IN FEBRUARY OF 2012, MY JOB relocated our family from northeast Oklahoma to East Texas. We had always lived in the country and always had animals. Unfortunately, we had to make the move quickly, and a home in the area with any amount of land, not to mention barns, was near nonexistent, or at least way too expensive.

So I found us a nice home in the suburbs. It was in a nice neighborhood, sat on a large acre lot—it was spacious and beautiful. We moved in, made it a home, and enjoyed it. But something was missing. That country lifestyle we'd all grown up in just wasn't there. We wanted to hear the horses whinny from the pasture, to smell the honeysuckle blowing in the breeze, to look out our door and see the animals playing, but to not see a neighbor in sight.

We had to get out of the burbs. We found a fixer-upper exactly four miles away on a nice piece of ground with seven acres, an arena, and two barns. The house wasn't as nice as what we'd been living in, but we could work on it. And most importantly, it wasn't in the burbs.

Now that we had all this room, with land and barns—what were we going to do? It didn't take long for my animal-loving girls to conjure up all kinds of ideas. Every day—no, make that every hour— they had a new animal they wanted me to buy. They spent hours looking online at every kind of dog, cat, pig, goat, cow, and horse you could ever imagine (but no llamas).

I did my best to be somewhat open minded. After all, that's exactly why we chose to move out to the country in the first place. But at the same time, I wasn't ready to buy every animal on the East Texas Swap n' Shop website. I'd seen that Matt Damon *We Bought a Zoo* movie, which was entertaining, sure, but also pretty nerve racking.

But, eventually, I decided to play along. First, we were adopted by a male blue heeler dog who made himself very comfortable at our place. He was a handsome, polite fellow. He knew basic commands, even how to shake. Since I'd lost my canine companion several months back, I decided to give him a home. No one knew who he was, and he had no collar. He was lovingly referred to as "Dog." We enjoyed having him around. Unfortunately, I don't think he enjoyed us quite as much, because after a week, he ran away, never to be seen again. We were a little bummed, but I guess he was just a rambler.

Then the girls wanted a pig. No, silly, not your regular, everyday, run-of-the-mill pig. Nope, no way. Why spend $10 on a pig, when you can spend $175? We needed a spotted black-and-white micro-mini potbelly pig. And that's exactly what we got. Enter Maxwell. I'd shown pigs growing up, and frankly, I was never crazy about them, but that's what the girls wanted, so that's what we did.

When we brought Maxwell home, the girls fawned all over him. "Oh, he's so adorable!" "He's just the cutest thing I have ever seen!"

And it was true. He was adorable. His little pink nose and fat round belly would soften the hardest of men. But, as it turned out, he was also an accomplished escape artist. No amount of fencing could keep his fat little physique in the yard. Every time we turned around, he was gone. The first few times, he was easy to find, but on the fifth day, he disappeared and didn't come back.

We took to Facebook, texted and called friends and neighbors, drove up and down the road, screaming out the truck windows as we looked for Maxwell. And you know what? It worked! Someone on Facebook saw him down the road in a neighbor's backyard, trying to make romantic advances on, of all things, a basketball. When I got down there, I saw him, but the reality was Maxwell didn't want to be caught. And even though he was little and fat, he was as fast as a mongoose. Me, April, and the neighbor chased him around the deck, the pool, and the house for over an hour, and I said words I didn't even know I knew. Let me tell you, you've never really lived until you have chased a micromini potbelly pig all over God's creation trying to capture him with a fishing net. But we finally got him, although it didn't feel like a victory.

Next up, the girls wanted a goat. But, just like the pig before him, it couldn't be just a good old $20 goat. Oh, no. We needed a pygmy fainting goat. You know those cute little goats that get startled by loud noises and then faint? Yes, those. Again, yes, they're cute. And it is hilarious when you drive around the corner on the riding lawn mower and the goat gets scared and falls over, stiff as a board. I mean, it's super funny. But that little feller wasn't very friendly. The girls wanted something they could hug and love and squeeze and play with. He was pretty standoffish, so we started looking for yet something else. Something cuddly.

We settled on a kitty. He was an orphan, probably three months old when we got him. He was so friendly and cuddly and happy to have a home. He was perfect. We named him Goliath, and he and Gracee became instant best friends. He tolerated her rough handling and overzealous displays of affection. Not only did he tolerate them, but he actually seemed to enjoy it. The kitty was happy. Gracee was happy. Everyone was happy.

If everyone was happy, what more could we possibly need? Well, no farm is truly complete without a horse, right? I already had a quarter-horse mare named Banjo—I'd bought her from a place in Wisconsin—that I'd been boarding at a farm down the road, and she was pregnant. On April 15, Banjo gave birth to a healthy, lively baby boy. We named him Shooter, a pretty sorrel colt with a white star on his forehead. Thanks to the overbearing attention paid to him by all my girls, he quickly became a spoiled rotten brat. His every move, buck, kick, and whinny was adored and laughed at on a daily basis.

I was beginning to think our zoo, I mean farm, was pretty much complete. We had dogs, cats, pigs, goats, and horses. What more is there? Evidently the answer was chickens. April informed me that a real farm wasn't complete until you had some. My thought was, *Okay, I can handle a couple of chickens.* But then she informed me we couldn't just turn the chickens loose as I had planned to do. Oh, no. We needed to build a coop. But not just any coop. April had a picture of a coop with a chandelier in it. A chandelier. Inside a chicken coop. Yeah, I had no words.

I did ask April if she was serious. Did she really want me to build her a chicken coop with chandeliers and wall decorations inside of it? Yep. She was serious, and that's exactly what she wanted me to do. So I did what I always seem to do when my girls want something. I fuss and complain loudly about it for a while, and then I figure out a way to make it happen. I built the coop the way April had imagined, cut a hole in the wall, and built a pen outside. With every crazy suggestion she made, I'd sigh, mutter something under my breath, and roll my eyes—just like I'd seen my teenager do a million times.

But I did exactly what she asked. Because that's what I do. I'm the husband. I'm the dad. And even though I may think the things they want from me are silly, or even sometimes downright ridiculous, if it makes them happy—at the end of my day, that's all that matters. That's the story of our zoo, I mean, farm. Yes, the one with a chicken coop outfitted with a chandelier.

This Too Shall Pass

I LOVE ANIMALS. MY FAMILY'S attachment to four-legged creatures goes back several generations. My great-grandfather would tell us stories of himself as a youth, and just like my own stories, most involved an animal of some sort. Like when he was a young man working in a livery stable in Oklahoma. He didn't have enough money to buy his own horse, so he'd board other people's horses, and then at night he'd saddle up a horse and ride it all the way to Salina to go dancing. Then he'd ride it as hard as he could back to Locust Grove, some fifteen miles away, put it up, give it some feed and water, and have it waiting for the customer the next morning. Now, that's not exactly an honest thing to do, but it sure made for a good story. Another time, he caught a full-grown coyote in the wild, brought it back to the ranch, and attempted to domesticate it and make it a pet. FYI, that didn't go well for my grandpa. Or for the coyote. Those are just a few of the hundreds of stories he told us as children. And even though we'd likely heard all those stories multiple times, they were never any less entertaining, and more often than not, if you paid close attention, there was a lesson that could be learned.

I've always believed that we, as humans, can learn a lot by watching animals. Sometimes the lessons are small and simple, and other times they can be much more profound. Here's a good example of the latter. I had a rather significant life lesson pounded into me, whether I wanted it or not.

Our young quarter horse, Shooter, is really well bred and was growing into a very nice horse. Since the moment he was born, he was cuddled and babied and spoiled rotten. He's really less of a horse and more akin to a Labrador retriever. He's a big pet. He's gentle and calm and will normally allow me to do anything I want to do to him without so much as a flick of his ears. He trusts me implicitly and knows I would never hurt him. However, something happened. Something scary and traumatic. When Shooter was a colt, he got what is known simply as "choke." It's exactly what its name implies—he choked on beet pulp. Being the mischievous and ornery critter that he is, he broke into the feed room in the barn and got into some feed that is meant only for our girls' show pigs. The beet pulp got lodged in his throat, and he choked. Now, choking in horses is much different than for a human. When we choke, our airways are blocked. We turn purple and lose the ability to breathe. That is not the case for horses. Choking only blocks the esophagus. They can breathe just fine; they just can't swallow. So while ultimately it can cause some problems, it's not quite the death sentence for them that it is for us. Their biggest problem is that they panic. They absolutely lose their minds because they're scared.

When I saw what was happening, of course, I came immediately to Shooter's assistance. My whole purpose during those ninety minutes, until the vet could get there, was to try to make him calm, reassure him, and keep him from hurting himself. He bucked, he reared, he kicked. His eyes were wide, white with fear, and he was soaked with sweat dripping from his body. He jerked me around like a rag doll, and since he outweighs me by seven hundred pounds, there was really little I could do about it. He struck out at me with his front feet and connected on multiple occasions. I've got the bruises on my elbow and shin to prove it.

What he could not realize was that the biggest danger was not the choke itself, and it wasn't from the man standing beside him trying to help, even though he seemed convinced that I was there to do him harm. The most severe danger posed to him in all this was himself. If Shooter was able to lie down and roll, which is what he wanted to do, then we could begin to have some real problems. He could twist a gut and colic, which is deadly for horses. Or he could get hung up on the fence next to us and break a leg. Thankfully, none of that happened. The vet arrived, stuck a tube the size of a water hose up Shooter's nose, and pumped warm water into him that cleared the blockage. The entire process took twenty minutes, but it probably seemed a lot longer to my anxious horse.

My point is that Shooter had taken a manageable problem and turned it into a serious situation because he panicked and overreacted. How many times in life can we say the same about ourselves? Too many times I see people, including myself, go through difficult times—whether it be the breakup of a relationship, the loss of a job, or any other number of things—and even though those are certainly significant circumstances, they are not circumstances that will kill us, no matter how convinced we are they will. We can overcome those problems. We can beat them. We just need to calm down, take a few deep breaths, allow those around us to help, and most of the time, everything will be all right. It's scary. It almost feels like the end of the world, but it's not. I kept telling Shooter, "This'll pass." And it did.

Chicken Farming 101

APRIL IS AN ANIMAL LOVER TOO. A true animal lover. Her heart is immediately filled with waves of joy when she sees a fluffy, clumsy, cuddly puppy playing with a tennis ball or a curious, rambunctious kitten attacking a ball of yarn or a reflection on the wall. You can almost see any stress or tension that may have shown on her face only moments before nearly instantly disappear.

She has been this way most of her life. When we were only small children, we lived just down the road and up the hill from each other. We rode bus number five to school. She got on in the mornings just before I did, and I got off the bus each day just after she did. Every day when the bus would drop her off at the end of their driveway, you could look around the property at their home and see any number of exotic animals grazing in the pastures. And it wasn't just dogs and cats. April's family had horses, buffalo, bobcats, mountain lions, peacocks, ferrets, goats, and countless other species and breeds of animal. So with her upbringing, it's easy to see how she would grow up to be an adult with a soft spot for animals. But still, there are a few animals she tends to hold in a higher regard than others, sort of a trinity, if you will. Horses, followed closely by dogs, and then there are chickens. She absolutely *loves* chickens. She loves to watch them peck around the yard for food. She loves to hear them talking to each other out in the yard and the rooster crowing at the start of each day. And she loves all the different breeds, varieties, and colors that are available. Chickens just make April happy.

One of her first memories as a child involves chickens. Unfortunately, it's not one of her favorite memories. Nearly thirty years later, it still haunts her. As a little bright-eyed seven-year-old, she grabbed an armful of her new baby chicks that her stepfather had bought for her. Against her mother's wishes, she snuck them into her bedroom, played with them until she got sleepy, then tucked them into bed with her and fell asleep hugging them closely against her body. Sadly, the next morning, she awoke to a scene from *Of Mice and Men*. Just like Lennie, she had cuddled and squeezed and loved the baby chickens too much. She had crushed them during the night. Unfortunately, there were no survivors.

I sometimes wonder if that tragic night so many years ago is what fuels her love for chickens now. She enjoys them more than you could imagine. When we first moved to our new property, we were so excited with all the possibilities. We had land and barns and room to do things we hadn't been able to do when we lived in town. April quickly had a plan. No sooner had we moved into our house than she was out tearing out junk and old shelving from a toolshed in the backyard. She gave me a picture of what she wanted it to look like inside, and when I had finished with my little Bob Vila project, she had what I would call the fanciest chicken coop in East Texas. It's the one I mentioned earlier, the one with a chandelier. If April ever decides to kick me out of the house, it's nice to know I have a pretty, frilly, and comfortable pad I can crash at until I am back in her good graces.

Once the chicken coop was complete, it was time for her to start adding some new tenants. Our first chicken purchases were just some run-of-the-mill leghorns. White bodies with red combs on their heads, they are the most common chicken you will find. While April was happy to have them, she yearned for more variety, more color. A woman in a small Texas town some thirty miles away had dozens of varieties of chickens running wild on her property. She invited April out to look around. I volunteered to drive her out there, which turned out to be much more of an undertaking than I had anticipated. It was truly in the middle of nowhere. April got some very vague directions to the chicken property, and of course, we got lost. Once we had made multiple U-turns, we finally found our way to the right place. April looked around in awe at the chickens scouring the landscape. They were everywhere, and she was in heaven. We quickly found just what she was looking for. She got two dominickers and one black banty. They were small but pretty. She happily scooped them up and put them in the pet taxi we had brought, and we headed home. All the way back she talked excitedly about the beautiful flock she now had. She was ecstatic at the thought of having to gather fresh eggs every day.

Months passed by, and the chickens began to mature. The anticipation of them laying eggs was almost unbearable for her. Every day she'd make her way out to the coop looking for eggs, and finally, it happened. Her first egg! You would have thought she had won the Indy 500, judging by the celebration she was having. Then the next day, there were more. And April's cup, it overflowed.

As the chickens got bigger, we began to notice that one of the dominickers looked a little different than the others. Bigger, thicker, and more aggressive. It was a rooster. But that was okay. One rooster wasn't a big deal. But then, the other dominicker began to get bigger too. And thicker, and more aggressive. It was a rooster too. I had always heard that two roosters meant trouble. But they had been together since birth and had always gotten along, so it shouldn't be any trouble, right? Unfortunately, no. That's not correct. You are going to have big trouble. One rooster clearly had the upper hand. He was bigger, stronger, faster, and more aggressive than the other. Sadly, before we even had the opportunity to separate them, nature ran its course. And once again, I saw this thirtysomething woman turn into a sad little girl right in front of my eyes. I disposed of the smaller rooster, hugged and kissed her, and told her I was sorry. And then I did what any good daddy and/or husband would do. I bought her more chickens.

Are we great chicken farmers? Goodness no. Do I get unbelievably tired of having to clean chicken mess off of my porch every single day? Yes. Do I kind of want to kill the big rooster when he sits right outside my bedroom window and crows at 6:00 a.m. every

Saturday morning? Yes. But as long as these stinkin' birds keep putting that smile on April's face, I suppose I will keep that chicken farmer out in the middle of nowhere on speed dial. Because what I hope is that our daughters are watching. And I hope they see that a man who loves them will do for them whatever is needed, whatever is asked, no matter how silly they may find it to be (like putting a chandelier in a chicken coop). Because they deserve that kind of respect and that kind of love. That's not to say I am perfect. Far from it. But they know, without a shadow of a doubt, that I love their mama to death. And I certainly hope they each find a man someday to love them as much as I love her.

Beautiful Chaos

THE COWBOY WAY OF LIFE has been ingrained in my family for a very long time. I was the fifth generation of ranchers on the Rocking S Ranch, which would later be known simply as Stamper Ranch. We showed a lot of horses, pigs, and even a few cattle through the years. We judged horses and livestock and gave speeches in our FFA programs. We built fence for folks in town and delivered truck-loads of feed for the old cattle farmers down the road who couldn't haul it for themselves anymore. Very few kids have been more involved in 4-H and FFA than me and my siblings. I admit I didn't always love it. As a child, it was a lot of hard work, a lot of long hours out feeding and washing and clipping and tending to sick animals. I didn't get to go play quite as much as some of my friends.

My dad is a softhearted man, kind and gentle for the most part. But when it came to working with the animals, he became a different man. Inevitably tempers flared, voices were raised, and feelings were hurt. Now, don't take that as bad as it sounds. In the whole scheme of things, this was "family time," and it was fun, in a weird way. There was this strange synergy we had. Even though emotions were tense and more than a few tears were often shed, we still laughed, and we made these amazing memories that we continue to laugh about today, some twenty-five years later. They are my favorite memories with my family.

As I've grown older, I've come to realize what a blessing it was to be able to grow up in the country surrounded by trees and hayfields and pastures full of horses and cows. To breathe in the cool spring air and smell the fresh-cut hay and hear the bawling of a new pen of calves in the corner lot. But more than all that, the time I spent with my family out there—in the winter, in the rain, snow, and sleet, or in the smoldering heat of an Oklahoma summer—was so much more. They are the fondest memories of my life. They are my most prized possessions and something that no one can ever take away.

I spent eighteen wonderful years on that ranch. Then I used all I had learned in 4-H and FFA and agriculture and was able to receive a full-ride scholarship to college. I spent the next four years engaging in extracurricular activities that would not have pleased my strict cowboy grandfather in the slightest bit. But then again, I did have something he had never had: a college diploma. And then right out of college, I got a good job with a decent salary, and my company put me on the road. For nearly fifteen years, I worked all over the country and in Canada. I traveled nearly three hundred days a year. I spent more time in airports, train stations, rental cars, and hotels than I could count. At first, it was fun. The country boy goes to the city. I spent a good bit of time in New York, Detroit, Boston, Toronto, Montreal, and Chicago. Places I never thought I'd visit. I loved it and became a professional traveler. I knew every restaurant or bar that was the place to be. I may have been the life of many parties, but that kind of killing time was killing me. I had gotten far away from my ranching roots. Such thoughts take me back deep in my memory.

But I am suddenly yanked back to reality by the screams of a teenage daughter. The pigs are loose and have scattered. They are just babies and haven't had a lot of time to get gentled down just yet. Abby is wearing Carhartt overalls and rubber mud boots, clearly not the most conducive outfit to running sprints and chasing pigs, but she's doing her best. And right on cue, the dad comes out in me, and I begin to yell and gripe and bark orders at her. She yells, "I'm trying!" as she rolls her eyes at me and continues to try to get these wild animals back in their pen. April and the girls and I finally get all four of them back in the barn and almost to their pen when one of them makes a break for it. He shoots through a gap and runs for the large door. Abby sees where he's headed and starts her chase after him. Just as she gets to the door, within arm's reach of the pig, her toe catches the water hose that is coiled on the ground. Her feet are way too far behind her, and there is no chance of her catching herself from this fall. April and I watch in slow motion as she hits the ground chest first. It draws a guttural *ugh* sound from her lungs on impact. And at that precise moment, I forget all about the pigs, I forget about the one that was quite possibly running as fast as he could for the highway. Instead, I focus solely on laughing at Abby. It's the funniest thing I have ever seen. She's not hurt, of course. As a matter of fact, the pig we were chasing has grown pretty curious as to what we're laughing at as well, so he comes walking back up to us and then right into his pen as if nothing ever happened. It's chaos. Beautiful chaos. And April, Abby, Emma, and I laugh the rest of the evening.

Twenty years from now, the girls probably won't remember too much about these pigs. They probably won't remember how they placed at the shows or how much money they won. But I can guarantee you this: they'll never forget the time Abby face-planted in the barn while chasing that crazy Berkshire hog.

Flew the Coop

NOT LONG AGO, MY LOVELY WIFE made a horse trade. She does this occasionally, and it's an adorable trait. She wheels and deals and sometimes even makes a good one. This was one of those times. She traded a miniature horse we had named Sparky for two smaller miniature horses. You see, April is a photographer, and a good one if I do say so myself. She does a lot of minisessions with children. And one of her most popular minisessions is with a real live unicorn. Yep, you read that right, she gives little girls a chance to dress up as their favorite storybook princess and take a picture with a living, breathing unicorn. Okay, it's not really a unicorn. It's a miniature horse with a glittering cone strapped to his head, gold spray paint on his feet, and colorful hair extensions. But to these little girls, he is a magical creature.

Well, if you're going to take such pictures, you need your own unicorn. So she bought Sparky. He was a good horse but not exactly the unicorn she was wanting. So she made a trade for these two others. They were a little smaller and just what she was looking for. One of them was a red dun. He is a little older and still a stallion. He will undoubtedly make a perfect unicorn someday. We decided to name him Dink.

The other one is only four months old. He was weaned right before we got him, and he was really missing his mama. A lot. It was sad to hear him cry and neigh for his mother. Emma, who was eleven at the time, was in the stall with him nearly all day the first few days we had him, playing with him and rubbing on him. She did her best to make him feel at home on our little farm. One of these times, she made a mistake. A horrible mistake. She didn't shut the gate behind her. Being that he was still pretty nervous and anxious in his new home, when he saw an open gate, like any unicorn, he made a break for it. Interesting fact number 1: a scared baby pony can run as fast as a cheetah chasing a gazelle. I'm not even kidding. He was like a little pint-sized rocket shooting across our field. Interesting fact number 2: I am *not* as fast as a cheetah chasing a gazelle. It was like a race between Dale Earnhardt Jr. in his NASCAR and me trying to keep up on a tricycle.

The race (or chase) wasn't even close. I was easily one hundred yards behind him within a matter of two seconds, and he wasn't slowing down. I was, however. I couldn't have been sweatier. And the little guy was gaining ground with every new stride. I hollered back at April, "Go get my rope!" So she headed back to the barn to get it, while I continued in pursuit of the tiny runaway.

Although I was clearly losing steam, the pony wasn't. In fact, he caught another gear like he'd been hit in the hind end with a hotshot. Little dude was gone like the Road Runner. Interesting fact number 3: fences mean absolutely nothing to a horse the size of a small dog. They can go through a fence, or under it, without even the slightest hesitation. He never broke stride.

Meanwhile, the neighbors have a new dog that did not approve of my presence on their property. He was all over me, but I was too tired to even care. If he bit me, he just bit me. My legs were mostly numb anyhow, so it shouldn't even hurt.

Finally, once the dog realized that I appeared to be suffering from emphysema or some other lung malfunction and was no danger to anyone, he went back home. I went on back to another house behind the neighbors, and there stood the little pony. Smug, smiling at me, it seemed, as he ate grass by their propane tank. But more important, he was standing still. Oh, thank God. I eased up on him like a mongoose on a cobra, walking ever so gently, although I'm sure my incessant wheezing wasn't helping my sneakiness. I got within ten feet of him, and now April was coming up behind me. She couldn't find my rope. Well, that's just dandy.

I was quietly talking to the colt, and he was just staring at me. I inched closer . . . closer . . . closer . . . and he made a run for it. I hurled my body at him and, somehow, caught him by the front leg. You may think to yourself, *Oh good! He caught him. It's over.* No way.

Interesting fact number 4: a tiny pony may be small in stature, but it is still as strong as André the Giant.

He hit me full force. Our heads butted. I bit my lip. I moaned. He jerked back. I fell forward. I grabbed another leg and finally wrestled him to the ground. Again, here I go with the wheezing and sweating. I actually feared for a moment that I was suffering from a massive myocardial infarction. I held on with all the strength I had left, and finally he stopped fighting. I had won. Either that or he had died under my weight. But no. He whinnied. He struggled a bit more but apparently realized I would sooner die than let go of him at this point. It was a mighty long walk back to our barn. As we approached the house, Emma was sitting on the porch swing. She said, "Sorry, Stoney." I'm not sure I replied, but it was less out of aggravation and more out of my continued heavy breathing and possible cardiac issues.

April walked up to us and said, "That little guy sure flew the coop, didn't he?" We chuckled and looked at each other and knew she had just named our newest unicorn addition to the farm: *Coop.*

A Predator in the Night

ALTHOUGH MY FAMILY SAYS I have a tendency to exaggerate things a tad, it would not be an exaggeration for me to say that some of the things that happen in our house are certainly out of the ordinary. When you put a group of five eccentrics like us into one house, you're bound to have some pretty crazy stories.

As the man of the house, I am the official protector of all things on the farm. The girls feed the animals and love them and care for them, and I make sure they don't get killed. Our neighbors have dogs that like to visit on occasion, plus there is a fox that lives nearby, and of course the occasional possum likes to sneak in and eat eggs.

Not long ago, we had an intruder. I was already in bed when suddenly I heard our backyard gate rattle loudly. I sat straight up and listened closely. Then I heard our young basset hound bawl as our chickens started squawking and carrying on. At 1:00 a.m., this is never a good combination. Something was definitely out there, and as official protector, I had a job to do. I jumped up out of bed, ran to the gun cabinet, grabbed my .22, and then headed toward the chicken coop.

The moon was huge that night and the yard brightly lit. To my surprise, I saw a coyote lying on his belly and slowly creeping up to the chicken coop. I yelled and immediately headed his way, leveling my gun on him. Of course, my scream startled him and he took off like a shot. I quickly surveyed my landscape, mostly to make sure there were no horses in my line of fire, and then took a shot. Judging by the yelping, I hit him, but he never missed a beat. In fact, he seemed to pick up speed as he ran away. By this time, I was standing beside our back porch. Our hound dog, the ferocious beast that he is (not), had apparently hidden underneath it. Startled by the gunshot, I assumed, he burst from underneath the porch bawling once again, from fear or bravado no one can be sure, running into my legs and getting tangled up in my feet.

Doing my very best not to trip and fall, I stepped hard to the right to catch myself and promptly stomped my bare foot directly onto a patch of sticker burrs that immediately turned my skin into a slice of swiss cheese. I felt at least ten thousand thorns suddenly in my sole (maybe not ten thousand), and with each step I took, they pushed deeper and deeper into my skin. So there I stood, the great protector, in my underwear (forgot to mention that), barefoot, bleeding, limping, and stepping on more stickers, carrying a gun and using my phone as a flashlight. It wasn't a pretty picture, but the chickens were safe for one more night.

I hobbled back inside, picked as many stickers out of both feet as I could (ten thousand is a lot to pull out), put the gun up, and climbed gently back into bed. I found my darling wife dead asleep and snoring. She hadn't moved one inch and had absolutely no clue as to the bravery and courage I displayed to save her chickens. But sometimes that's how it is for protectors—you save the day, and nobody knows but you and the chickens. And that hound dog.

Doc

DOC WAS MY AUSTRALIAN SHEPHERD. He was coming up on his fourteenth birthday in March of 2014. He had been with me at nearly every step of my adult life, and that's not an exaggeration. I got him when I was twenty years old, and in those fourteen years, I rarely went anywhere without him. He loved nothing more than hopping up in the back of the truck and riding down the road with the wind blowing through his long, pretty hair while his eyes, one blue, one brown, filled with delight. He went with me to the store, to visit friends, to visit family. He went with me to the East Coast, to the West Coast, and to Canada. To most people, seeing me was synonymous with seeing Doc.

Recently, I loaded Doc in the back of that truck for the very last time. I found what I had been dreading to find for the better part of a year—my best old buddy lying stretched out in the yard, soaking up the sun, as he so often liked to do. He had gotten quite deaf in his old age, so when I called his name from the porch and he didn't move, I just thought he was enjoying his nap in the sunshine. However, when I got down to him, I realized that my sweet friend was gone. He had crossed over Jordan's stormy banks. He had bumped my hand with his head, asking me to pet him, for the very last time. I'd never look in the rearview mirror again to see his pretty face, literally smiling, as we drove down the road. He'd never lie at my feet as I played my guitars, as my biggest fan. The most constant presence in my adult life was gone. And for that, I am terribly sad.

I got Doc in May of 2000 when he was nine weeks old. He was an adorable little fuzzy ball of fur. I'm not usually what you would consider a dog person. I grew up on a horse ranch. I've seen a lot of animals come and go. I've seen them be bought, sold, and traded. And I've seen them die. I think that probably caused me to be a little callous toward animals at times. I never got too close. Except for Doc.

He and I had an instant connection. I saw him for the first time before his eyes were even opened, and I knew I wanted him. When I got him, he was like a little teddy bear. He was so cute and fun to play with. The first night at my house, he was scared. So I picked him up, set him on my belly, and he went to sleep. It was like a bond formed from that very second. We made an agreement. I'd take care of him, and he'd take care of me. He never needed a leash. Wherever I was, he was there, right beside me.

Doc loved the Frisbee, or a ball, or a stick. Or really anything else I could throw for him to fetch. He was so proud each and every time he brought it back to me. Thousands of times, no doubt. One day, when Doc was only about a year and a half old, we were at the ranch and gathering a herd of buffalo off the back pasture so we could work our horses. We had a bull in the herd that was a tad snorty, and for some reason unbeknownst to me, Doc decided to take him head on. He ran up behind him and bit him on the back leg. When he did, that bull kicked out hard and caught Doc right on the bridge of the nose. His entire body flew through the air, flipping head over heels and landing in a pile about twenty feet away. Unfortunately, when you live on a working ranch that uses a lot of dogs, you see this happen from time to time. It's sad, but you just have to move on. But I *loved* Doc. I ran my horse over to him and jumped down beside him. He was stretched out on his side; a flap of skin had been peeled off the bridge of his nose and was lying over his eye. He was breathing, so it hadn't snapped his neck, as I had feared. I picked him up and laid him over the swells of my saddle. I rode over to my house, which was just over the hill and across a pasture. I carried him up on my porch and assessed the damage. I was scared he wouldn't make it, but he was still breathing okay and didn't act like any particular bones were hurting, and he wasn't crying. So I doctored him up, cleaned up the wound, and superglued that piece of skin back across his nose. I put some water and food down in front of him. Doc stayed on that porch for three days, seemingly improving every day. Then on the fourth day, he stood up, shook off, and followed me to the barn. He didn't miss another beat. He carried that scar across his nose for the rest of his life, but he never bit another buffalo, that I can promise you.

For fourteen years, he was my partner. He lived with me in

Oklahoma, Florida, Virginia, Oklahoma again, and Texas. Through hurricanes, tornadoes, earthquakes, droughts, and floods. He's seen me skinny, fat, mad, happy, and sad. He knew me with hair, and now without. And none of that mattered to him in the slightest. He liked me when I was pretty hard to like. He even liked me when I didn't like myself, and he was happy to see me every single time he set eyes on me. If we could all have the same kind of attitude he had, and the short memory to be able to forget the bad that happened yesterday and think only of today, what a wonderful world this would be.

I think John Grogan, author of *Marley and Me,* said it best: "A dog has no use for fancy cars or big homes or designer clothes. . . . A waterlogged stick will do just fine. . . . A dog doesn't care if you are rich or poor, educated or illiterate, clever or dull. Give him your heart and he will give you his." How many people can you say that about? How many people can make you feel rare and pure and special? How many people can make you feel extraordinary?

I sure do miss you, Doc.

You're a Doll

I KNOW SAYING *life is hard* is terribly cliché. But let's be honest, most clichés are clichés because they're true. And I can think of nothing more true than *life is hard*. That doesn't mean it's always hard. Quite the contrary, actually. Life is an ever-changing landscape of peaks and valleys. Sometimes it feels so easy, when it's filled with happiness and colors and laughter and beauty. These good things are what keep us going during the hard times and during the sad times. It's important to remember these wonderful and happy things when the going gets tough or when things aren't so rosy.

And then sometimes the hard times are downright tragic. It's heartbreaking to see others who have to endure tragedy such as car accidents or losing loved ones to sickness and disease well before their time. Other times life simply runs its course—naturally. Every race has its finish line, I suppose. And from where my family stands, my grandfather's finish line isn't so far away. His race is nearly run.

I have been pretty fortunate in my life. I haven't suffered any real tragedies involving my family or close friends. I haven't lost any immediate family to sickness. Only twice in my thirty-five years have I lost someone close to me. In 1992, I lost my granny Stamper to Lou Gehrig's disease, and in 2001 my great-grandpa died just one month shy of his 105th birthday. Yes, you heard me right, 105 years old. And he got married when he was 104. True story. So this is fairly new territory for me. For all of us.

My grandfather Claude Stamper, whom I always called Papa, was born and raised on my family's ranch in Murphy, Oklahoma. It's right between Chouteau and Locust Grove, four miles off of Highway 412. It's the only place he's ever known. His mama and daddy lived there and died there. He raised his four boys there with my sweet granny. My dad and his brothers raised all of us there. And now we've got the youngest generation of Stampers on the ground. Some of them live on the ranch, some off, but still in the same lifestyle to which we were all accustomed. The lifestyle my papa and my great-granddad provided for us.

Sometimes growing up that way didn't seem so awesome. When most of my friends went home from school to play video games or just do nothing at all, we were busy cleaning stalls, warming up and cooling down horses, and feeding and bathing horses, cattle, pigs, and sheep. It was a lot of work. It didn't seem like a blessing at the time, but looking back on it now, that's exactly what it was. We were taught a strong work ethic. But we weren't made to work while the adults sat in the air-conditioning. They led by example—work hard and do your best. My dad, papa, and even great-granddad would work from the time the sun came up until it went down.

When my great-granddad (we called him Granhappy) had gotten too old to work for our house-moving company, he took up carpentry. He spent his twilight years building some of the most awful carpentry projects you've ever seen in your life. But it didn't matter to him. He just needed to work. And besides, he couldn't see well enough to know it was crooked and ugly.

I get a bit misty eyed, reminiscing about those times spent with Granhappy and with Granny and Papa Stamper. Those times feel like so long ago, but their voices are still so clear, as though they're in the other room. My granny calling my papa "Claudie." Granhappy and his wife, Dorothy, singing "Come and Dine" at church on Sundays. The memories are fresh and vivid. My papa patting Granny's knee and saying to me, "Stone, ain't she just the purtyest thang you ever seen?" And the answer was "Yes, she is." She was so kind and gentle. So meek and mild. But she could ask for anything in her soft and sweet voice and he would move mountains to make it happen. He loved her with all his heart.

After forty-four years of marriage, she succumbed to the complications of ALS on December 28, 1992. It was a hard blow for our whole family. But even more so for my papa. He had lost his best friend, his confidante, his "pardner." His life was changed forever. On the day she died, I spent the night with him at his house—it felt so big, so empty. Then the next night, I stayed again. And then again the next night. I had inadvertently become roommates with my papa. We were like a couple of lame college kids living together. He didn't know how to cook, and I didn't either. We had coffee and toast every morning, until I learned how to make eggs and bacon without catching anything on fire. My mom or my aunt or my cousin came and did laundry for us until we learned how to do that too. Papa liked to bake brownies, and he did so nearly every day. He was glad I was there, and I was glad to be with him. I watched him and listened to his wheeling and dealing on the phone. He was selling, or buying something to sell, every time he talked to someone, and I got my first sales lessons just sitting around and listening to him.

Those were lessons that would serve me well and mold me into the man I am today. As time passed, he needed me less and less, but the bond we built in that year and a half is one that we still share today. I love him. I know he's not perfect, but he's funny, generous, and a great storyteller. But he can be strict and very hard on people, which just so happen to be traits that I possess. Granny was the perfect yin to his yang. She was the perfect mellow to his hard edges. After she died, he never remarried. Oh, he had some girlfriends. But he never married again. I guess he thought he couldn't do any better than he had done with Clarice June Plake. And I agree.

His last few years have been hard ones for him. A small, withered body now stands where a once big, strong man stood. His voice was loud and boisterous, but it's now weak and muffled. His old legs are bowed from too many horses, and not long ago, he fell and broke his hip. He's had surgery and has had some complications. He lost a lot of blood, and not enough oxygen made its way to his brain. His mind was slipping even before the accident. He'd call me every evening wanting me to come over and drink coffee with him. Something I would have gladly done had I not lived in Texas, more than six hours away. Something he forgot every time he called.

When I put my selfish feelings aside for a moment and remember how badly he misses my granny, how long he's gone without feeling her hand in his or hearing her sweet, soft voice whisper his name, then, and only then, do I feel a sense of joy wash over me. Although I'm not always a good example of one, I am a Christian, and I do believe in heaven. My grandmother has been there for nearly twenty-two years. Just waiting on him. And on the day they are reunited, I'd give nearly anything to see their faces when their eyes meet. Oh, what a day of rejoicing that will be. It makes me want to let him know it's okay. "Papa, you can go now. You've taught us all you know. You've given all you can give. We'll be okay. Go see Granny, and we'll see you sometime soon."

I wanted to tell him these things as I reached down over his hospital bed to hug him and kiss his head. But instead, I just said, "I love you *so* much." And with a sparkle of recognition in his eye, he looked at me and mumbled something he'd said a million times before to me and my siblings and cousins: "I love you, honey. You're a doll."

Back in My Day

As we sat in our living room one evening, I looked around at my family, and this is what I saw. My then thirteen-year-old watching videos on her laptop and playing *Minecraft* on the iPad. I saw the nine-year-old playing countless different games on her iPod while texting her cousins, aunts, uncles, grandparents, and maybe even April and me from the other room, if the mood struck. I saw my wife looking at Pinterest and Smith County Swap and Shop on Facebook on her iPhone. And of course, I watched all of this as I sat in my recliner and did some weekly reports for work and worked on my latest blog, while simultaneously checking Facebook and ESPN Score Center for football scores. It made me really sit back and realize the stark differences between the world I grew up in, the world my parents and grandparents grew up in, and the world the girls are now growing up in.

I, like most kids, always rolled my eyes at the ever-so-repetitive "when I was your age" stories told by my dad and my granddads. Sure, they were generally pretty entertaining stories. The first few times, anyway. But once you had heard them talk about walking nine miles to school in two feet of snow, barefoot, uphill, carrying their baby brother on their back, and whatever else kind of wild details they may add each time, I just sort of began to zone out as soon as I heard the words "When I was your age" or "Back in my day." First of all, we don't commonly get two feet of snow in Oklahoma. And it's pretty dang flat, with not many hills in sight. I even know exactly where the school was, and there is not a single hill between here and there. And why was everyone always barefoot? We aren't talking about the Ice Age here. I've seen pictures of them all when they were kids, and in every single picture they are wearing shoes. I made a point to look at their feet in every picture. I'm sorry, but I ain't buying it.

However, as I grow older myself, I begin to find myself not only thinking about how things are different now versus thirty years ago, but also giving the long, drawn-out speeches that often begin with phrases like "When I was a kid" or "When I was your age." I can hear myself doing it, and I hate it. I may as well start using Lucky Tiger hair tonic, getting my initials stitched onto the cuffs and collars of my neatly starched white oxford shirts, and eating at Denny's for three meals per day. Maybe I'll go ahead and flirt with the old waitress with the raspy, smoky voice, and she can call me "sweetie" and "baby," while she brings me my eggs over easy, with sourdough toast and strawberry jelly. Maybe a piece of apple pie for dessert, but not pecan, because the pecans get stuck in my dentures. Needless to say, I've spent a little time with the old man at Denny's.

Now, don't get me wrong, if I can grow to be as half as good of a man as my dad, my granddads, or my great-granddads, well, in the words of my granddad himself, I would be prouder than a peacock. He may also say, "I'd be puffed up as a stomped-on toad" (whatever in the world that means), or "swelled up like a poisoned pup," which is my favorite and always made me giggle like a little girl. Old cowboys really have a way with words. However you want to say it, I'd love to someday be the kind of man they are. But if I could be as good as they are, without having to pull the "back in my day" routine, well, that would be okay by me.

Unfortunately, I am finding it is impossible to try to get this point across without stooping to the old standby grandpa speech. Only now, all these years later, do I really understand why they felt the need to incessantly tell these stories. Everything begins to make a little more sense once you are on this side of the conversation. I've learned it can be exasperating to talk to a child from another generation than you, because they tend to look at you like you are asking them to go plow the fields with a mule or go milk the cows before school, when all you are truly doing is asking them to clean their rooms or take care of their dogs or do the dishes. They just don't seem to get it, and it's doubtful they ever will. Because the differences between each generation grow bigger and bigger each time. And the bad news is, each generation becomes a little bit lazier and gets a little more entitled.

Now, before you go to jumping all over me about calling your kids lazy or entitled, just hold on. I'm not saying anything bad about anyone's kids. All I am saying is, my great-grandpa worked harder than my grandpa, my grandpa worked harder than my dad, and my dad worked harder than me. The point of the "talk" is to ensure that our children understand that hard work is necessary for success. To understand that we are not asking them to do anything that we ourselves haven't done. And probably much more. Okay, so maybe we stretch the truth a tad and talk about our long, uphill, barefoot walks to school. Regardless, we only use it to try to get the best out of our kids.

It's important to me to teach my girls some of the finer points of cowboy logic that I had hammered into my little freckled noggin. They are things that will stick with me all my life. They've made me a better person. Here are a few of the more interesting pearls of wisdom straight from the old timers' mouths that I try to recite to myself often:

- "Life ain't given to you." (Simple enough.)
- "Don't squat with yer spurs on, but if you do, just get your legs out in front of you a little bit."
- "Never miss a good chance to shut up." (You'll likely never get better advice than that.)
- "Always take a good look at what you are getting ready to eat. It's not so important to know what it is, but it's critical to know what it was." (Food don't just 'happen,' people.)
- "Good judgment comes from experience, and a lot of that comes from bad judgment." (I'd say *most* of mine comes from bad judgment.)

- "If you find yourself down in a hole, why dontcha quit digging?" (I still haven't quite figured this one out yet.)

And last, but not least, my favorite:

- "Good luck tends to look a whole lot like hard work."

I think if we all spent a little time giving a little more tough, grandfatherly love to our kids instead of buying them every blasted thing they want and catering to them hand and foot, without making them work for it, we would likely be doing a service to everyone they come into contact with in their lives.

And, well, back in my day, that was just how it was done.

Murphy Church of God

AY THE LORD RICHLY BLESS YOU and keep you safely in his arms. Shake hands and be friendly. You're dismissed." How many times have I heard these words in my life? Thousands of times, no doubt. These were the words my grandfather, my mother's father, Brother Eugene Grace, used at the end of every sermon he preached. He was the pastor of Murphy Church of God in Murphy, Oklahoma, for the better part of fifty years. He moved to a few different churches across the state during that half century of work in the service of the Lord, but most of my life, he stood at the pulpit in that little country church in our tiny community of Murphy that consisted of no more than half a dozen families. The

Welcome to Murphy sign boasted a population of ninety-eight citizens, although as hard as I try, I cannot come up with more than half of that. Maybe if we included dogs, cats, sheep, and horses, but still, that's pushing it.

The attendance on a Sunday morning at our little church was generally more than the population on the sign. In fact, when I was younger, I remember the congregation being so big that you'd have a hard time finding an open spot on a pew. Church isn't normally considered a fun place for a child, but I admit that a Sunday morning service at our church had a certain amount of excitement to it. It was like a huge family reunion every single Sunday.

Both sides of my family, the Stampers and the Graces, attended Murphy Church of God. My uncle Rick was the leader of the youth group, a group that both my future wife, April, and I attended together as kids. My cousin Terry played the piano and led the music along with my mom and my aunt Marilyn. And my other grandpa, Papa Stamper, was the Sunday school superintendent. At the end of Sunday school every week, he would jerk the door open on each classroom, undoubtedly wearing one of his eternally cool and colorful blazers, and he'd call "Time!" letting us know it was time to move to the auditorium for the sermon. My brother, sister, cousins, and friends would talk and laugh as we made our way out into the sanctuary to find our seats as the old folks shook hands and chitchatted in the lobby. Inevitably, my grandmother, Sister Grace, would hunt me down to give me hugs and kisses, no matter how big or old I had gotten. She'd then take her place on the second row on the left side of the pews, with her arms spread out on the back of the bench and her eyes pointed to the heavens, and she'd sing every word to every song. All through the sermon she'd keep her eyes closed and repeat over and over again, "Praise God, praise God, praise God. Thank you, Jesus, thank you, Jesus, thank you, Jesus." She'd never stop saying it, and more importantly, you didn't want her to, because you knew she meant it. I always felt like maybe God listened to her just a little bit closer than he did anyone else. I always felt like if she was praying for me, nothing could ever go wrong.

On the other side of the sanctuary sat R. L. Stamper, my great-grandfather (Granhappy). Born in 1896 and hard as nails, he was a semifamous evangelist in northeast Oklahoma and western Arkansas. His silver hair combed straight back, a starched white shirt with the initials RLS stitched on the cuffs and collar, and either a blue or red sport coat and a tie to match. He left his cowboy hat on the hat rack by the front door. He was the definition of the fire-and-brimstone preacher you see on television. He was generous to a fault, always kind to everyone he met, but he could definitely scare you to death with his stories of the End of Days that he was certain were upon us. He would often have his own sermon, all by himself in the corner. His voice was loud and hoarse, and if you listened closely, you would often hear your own name in his prayers. Between his prayers and my granny's, there was no doubt in any of our minds that we were covered in God's blessings and protection. Oftentimes, during testimony, his testimony would turn into the sermon. Once the old man got rolling, he was like a freight train, and it took a while to slow him down. On extra-special Sundays, he and his wife, Dorothy, whom he married after my great-grandmother died, would get up in front of the church and sing the old gospel song "Come and Dine." "'Come and dine,' the Master calleth, 'come and dine.' You may feast at Jesus' table all the time." They never sang a different song that I recall, but they didn't need to. The funny thing about it was, neither one of them could sing worth a quarter. They were both off key, and neither of them in the same key. My cousin Terry would keep playing that piano as if he were playing for the Gaithers, and if one of them would hit an unusually flat note, which they would inevitably do, you could hear him giggle over the microphone but never miss a beat on the piano.

And then back to the pulpit stood my papa Grace. Small in stature, quiet in person, but behind the pulpit he was, and still is, a warrior. A warrior for God. I can honestly say that in my nearly forty years on this earth, there is not a preacher I'd rather hear deliver the Word of God than my papa. Sure, I know I am biased. But I also know good preaching when I hear it. And I have heard a lot of it. Twice on Sunday and every Wednesday night for eighteen years. Less often than that as an adult, but I still go and "get fed," as the old folks like to call it, every chance I get.

In fact, we made the six-hour trip back to Murphy not too long ago. The church is smaller now. The building is the same size, of course, but it seems smaller. And the congregation isn't nearly what it once was, but that doesn't mean they won't get the same message delivered to them as they would have if the crowd were bigger. It's funny how certain things, no matter how much time passes, never change, though. The distinct smell of the lobby and sanctuary, a mixture of cleaning supplies and thirty-year-old carpet. My cousin Terry's loud and flamboyant laugh echoing through the auditorium. The sound the doors make when my papa would lock them as everyone was leaving to go have lunch with the family. Those little details seemed pretty inconsequential, but it's pretty crazy just how important they are to me now that I'm a little older.

April and I raise our kids to believe just as we were taught to believe. We read the Bible, we say our prayers, and we do our best to spread goodness and kindness and generosity to all those who cross our path. We take them to church, but I have never been able to find a church I've felt the fondness for that I have for Murphy Church of God. That church has been a part of my family for more than ninety years. Our families were built there, many of us were married there, a few have nursed themselves back from divorce there. And many— more than I care to remember—have said goodbye there after they passed from this life into the next. And sadly, that number is growing. But no matter how many of the older generations we lose, still she stands—Murphy Church of God. It makes me sad that Murphy church is not a part of my weekly routine any longer. But one thing is for certain, just as my grandfather prayed over me each week from its pulpit and promised me he would, the Lord has richly blessed me.

Granny's Letter

AFTER A LONG AND DIFFICULT FIGHT against Alzheimer's disease, my papa Stamper finally went home to be with the Lord and my sweet granny. They had been apart for twenty-two years, since her death in 1992. We were very sad, of course. He was our rock. He led our family through thick and thin, and now he's gone. I had the privilege of reading a story I had written for him at his funeral. It was a celebration of a good man and a good life.

After the funeral service, we all made our way to his house. I felt closer to him just sitting in his dining room. He was always a snappy dresser, and he had some amazingly cool old vintage sport coats in his closet, and I was the only one in the family who would dare wear them. So I went into his closet and grabbed a few of my favorites.

While we were standing there, we began sifting through some of the stuff scattered on his desk. April found this handwritten letter, presumably written right after Granny found out she had been diagnosed with ALS, which would ultimately take her life. The paper is weathered and yellowed, and it's written in her perfect cursive writing. What a neat thing to find. And what a wonderful person, searching herself for strength so she could live for her boys. The thought of her sitting right at this same desk so many years ago, writing something so inspirational, gave me goose bumps. It had likely been right in that same spot for more than twenty years. And on this day, God chose to show it to me. On this difficult day, when we were wondering how life would go on without Papa in it, Granny showed us.

The letter reads,

I must not worry! I must not feel sorry for myself. I must not let these things destroy me. I must trust in the Lord and let him lead me and guide me. I must take my burdens to the Lord and leave them there; and not take them back up and worry. If I do, I will surely destroy myself.

I have so much to be thankful for and I must let my mind dwell on these things. I have a home, a fine home. And I have four of the finest sons that God ever created. I am so proud of them. I must live for them. They are reason enough for me to straighten my shoulders and lift my chin and look up.

I am not going to call back this incident in my life to look at it again. It is water under the bridge—gone on down to join a million, trillion other incidents until it loses its identity. It is no use to chase that which has disappeared. I must love and work with what I have at hand, and find peace and fulfillment of life.

What an amazing thing to find and read on that day. But what I could never have known at the time is how much it would help me at a later date. A few years after finding this note, I was in a terrible car wreck. I was injured very badly, and I still haven't fully recovered. But one day I again came across this note. And that final sentence continues to push me to be better, to get stronger, to not let the devil win this battle that he hurled at our family. *I must love and work with what I have at hand, and find peace and fulfillment of life.* Perfect words from my sweet grandmother, some twenty-five years later. As long as I live, I know I will never receive a more blessed gift than this note of strength and courage from her.

The Old Man
and Strawberry Jelly

"RISE AND SHINE, STONE! Coffee's hot; biscuits are on!" I can still hear my grandfather's loud, boisterous voice bellowing through his big house. Every morning, just like clockwork, he'd wake me up at 6:00 a.m. with these words. It was actually fairly generous of him to allow me to sleep until six, because he'd already been up for an hour or so by that time. But he liked that first hour by himself each morning. He'd put the coffee on, take a shower, and get dressed, with the exception of his starched dress shirt that had the initials CWS stitched into the cuff. He'd wait to put that on until he'd finished with his breakfast. So each day, when I first saw him after waking up, he'd be wearing a tight white undershirt, his legs crossed, drinking his coffee from a cup and matching saucer, and reading the Bible. Every day.

I'd take a quick shower and get dressed, then join him in the dining room by 6:15, because when you are a thirteen-year-old boy, it doesn't take too long to get ready. We had our timing so precise that when I came into the dining room each day, the biscuits would be ready to come out of the oven. I'd tell him, "Good morning," and he'd answer, "Good mornin', honey." I'd pour my own cup of coffee and then take the biscuits out and set them on top of the stove. Then I'd get out the butter and strawberry jelly. I loved our mornings together. We had our routine down pat. But it wasn't always that way. Let me back up a tad.

When I was eleven years old, my grandmother, Clarice June, began having trouble with her leg. At first, the doctors thought she had a pinched nerve, but after some more testing, we discovered that it was much more serious. She had ALS, more commonly known as Lou Gehrig's disease. The disease was swift. In just two years it had taken over her body. On December 28, 1992, after spending the Christmas holiday in Saint Francis Hospital in Tulsa, her suffering finally ended. Our family was lost, but it was much harder on my grandfather. They had been married for forty-four years, and together since high school. Even though we had all known this day was coming, we really didn't seem as prepared for her being gone as we should have been. That night we went to Papa's house to sit with him. The whole family was there. My loud family was eerily silent. It seemed that all the air had been taken out of us. Later, as everyone began to pack up and leave, I asked Papa if he'd want me to stay with him. He smiled for the first time in days and said, "Well, sure!" I told my mom and dad I was going to stay with him, and they said that was fine.

The next morning, I heard him toiling around in the kitchen. I heard cabinet doors slamming and pots and pans rattling and banging together. I walked in to find him opening a can of biscuits. The coffee was already made. I asked, "Do you need any help?" He said, "Good mornin', honey! Nope, I got it under control. Go get you a shower, and I'll have it ready when you're done." I did as I was told, but when I came back into the kitchen, there was a cloud of smoke hovering near the ceiling, and on the stove sat a pan of burnt black biscuits. He said, "Mighta left 'em in a minute or two too long." I laughed at him and said, "You reckon?" He said, "Ain't nothing that some butter and strawberry jelly can't fix," and then we sat down at the table to have one of the more memorable breakfasts I've ever had. An old man, a young boy, a plate of burnt biscuits, and a conspicuously empty chair where only a few days ago my grandmother had sat. Neither of us really knew what to say, which was an uncommon issue for both of us. As I watched my papa slather his burnt biscuit with butter and strawberry jelly, he quietly said, "Lord, I miss her." I tried to say something, but I knew if I even opened my mouth the slightest bit, I wouldn't be able to control the crying that just bubbled near the surface. So instead, I nodded my head while staring blankly down at my plate. I fought back those tears with all my might and ate that burnt biscuit and strawberry jelly.

Over the next few weeks, I gradually moved more of my clothes and other needed items to Papa's house from my family's house, which was only a couple hundred yards across the pasture from us. I stayed with him every night. He needed me there, and it made me feel useful. On most nights, we'd go get dinner at a restaurant in town. My mom or my aunt or my cousin would come by a few times each week and do our laundry or clean around the house, and I did the dishes every night before bed. And then each morning, of course, we had our biscuits and jelly.

It always tickled me how much he enjoyed his jelly in the mornings. It wasn't some special brand. As a matter of fact, it didn't even really matter what brand it was, he'd eat it and act like it was the best thing he ever ate. Shoot, he'd even eat the little free packets of it that sat on the tables of the little greasy-spoon diners that he loved so much. It makes me wonder, Did he just like the taste, or was it something else? Was it because the taste or the smell of it took him back to another time? Maybe back to a picnic with my grandmother when they were young, or perhaps to an early-morning breakfast, sitting at his own grandpa's knee?

It's been over twenty-five years now since those mornings. Such a long time ago. But just a few Saturdays ago, I was sitting alone on the front porch, drinking my coffee, when my daughter Emma woke up and came out onto the porch where I sat. She said, "I'm going to cook some biscuits." About twenty minutes later, she came out onto the porch and said, "The biscuits are ready, if you want one, but I burned them a little bit." I grinned at her and said, "You know, my grandpa used to tell me, 'It's nothing that a little bit of butter and strawberry jelly can't fix.'"

Forever and Ever, Amen

THE GIRLS AND I WERE DRIVING home from Oklahoma on the Sunday after Thanksgiving. As I was driving, my thoughts kept going straight back to the ranch. To the large den in my grandparents' home, where we would play pool, watch football, talk about horses or the big buck we saw at the tree stand that morning and that we hoped to see again that evening. Then there was the smell of the food in the oven, and listening to my granny, mom, aunts, and cousins in the kitchen laughing and talking as the meal gets its final preparations. Just before we all pile in on the feast, we would hold hands and say a prayer of thanks, led by my grandpa, for all that we had.

When I think of this family that our grandparents built for us, it makes me feel proud. The bond a family has is stronger than any one person can ever be. Sure, there will be occasional spats. That's just family. But at the end of the day, our blood, our love for each other, and our appreciation for each other can overcome any problems we encounter.

We are all human. We all have the occasional hurt feelings. We all have selfish thoughts. We may all thoughtlessly utter an unkind word or even say something downright hurtful. But none of these things should ever be powerful enough to defeat a family that's been forged by the generations before us.

We may not always agree. We may even sometimes drive our family members crazy with bad decisions and stupid mistakes. I'm certain I have. But the whole point of having this family behind you is to forgive each other and to support each other. It's easy when everything is good. It's what a family does when faced with difficulty and trials that shows their true character. It makes me proud to be a part of a family that's been able to endure many of those difficult things and still can come together for a holiday and tell stories, laugh, play games, and just enjoy being around each other. It's something I love being a part of. It's something I love that I am able to give to my wife and daughters. It's better than any material thing I could ever give them.

And once the day was over, I felt a little sad, just as I have been every year that I can remember. But then I looked around the cab of the truck at the family that my wife and I have made. And I prayed I am able to teach them the value of a family, just as I was taught, so that they can someday teach it to their children. So that someday, when I'm an old, worn-out cowboy sitting in my rocker, looking around the room at the legacy I'm leaving behind, I can feel happy and confident that the family will go on being a family when I'm gone.

I'm thankful for so many things in my crazy life. I try to thank God each and every day. But what I will always be most thankful for is simple. It's family, always has been.

Epilogue

MY LIFELONG DREAM HAS BEEN to write a book. For most of my life, I've written just because I love to write. But it was always just for me. No one ever read anything I wrote until I created *The Daddy Diaries* on Facebook. Then I began to get a moderate following that seemed to enjoy my writing. It was exciting to have had a dream all my life of being a writer and then to find out that some folks actually liked my work. So when after four years of having the Facebook page I was approached by WaterBrook asking me if I would be interested in writing a book, I was absolutely elated. A dream come true. I was in a great place in my life. The best place I'd ever been, really. I had a beautiful, amazing wife who loved me, despite all my many faults. I had three daughters who believed there was nothing I couldn't do, and the simple sight of them would send my heart leaping. I had a great job in Texas and provided well for my family. It was a wonderful time in our lives. So in the summer of 2017, work on my book began. I began writing and compiling stories and making my first pass at putting a book together. It was crude, but it began to take shape. All was well.

Then November 8, 2017, happened. It was the worst day of my life. It was the worst day of my family's life. At about ten in the morning, I was driving to urgent care because I believed I was coming down with the flu. April was taking Gracee to school. I left shortly after and headed to town. It's pretty crazy how quickly one's life can go from perfect to possibly being over in just a split second. An Enterprise rental truck had pulled out into my lane at an intersection and come to a stop. The pickup in front of me had just a fraction of a second to get around it. I, however, wasn't so lucky. With cars on my right side and lots of oncoming traffic on my left, I had no options. I was driving the speed limit of sixty miles per hour when I hit the big truck sitting in my lane. It was like hitting a brick wall. I had never had a wreck before. Never even had an insurance claim. So this was a first-time experience for me. Upon impact, I vaguely remember the airbag hitting me in the face. But everything happened so fast, I wasn't sure if I was hurt. It turned out that I definitely was. I was pinned in the vehicle. A good Samaritan came running up to me and asked my name. I said, "My name is Stoney Stamper. Please tell my girls I love them." And then I passed out.

I was in and out of consciousness for the remainder of the near hour of being pinned in the vehicle. Only a few minutes after the wreck, April pulled up on the scene. She knew nothing about the wreck at that time. She was just coming home from taking Gracee to school. I can't even imagine the shock and horror of what she must have felt that rainy day in November—seeing my mangled body pinned in a truck, shaking, losing consciousness, screaming in pain. She got in the back seat behind the driver's seat, wrapped her arms around me from behind, and began to pray. I don't know all of what she said, but I remember this much: "Please don't take him from us, Lord. We need him. Please cover him in your protection." As she was praying, the firemen and emergency workers were trying to free me from the truck. My right arm was very clearly broken. My legs were pinned between the dash, which had completely caved in, and my seat. My left leg particularly was causing a great amount of pain. But because of the inability to actually see my legs, we didn't know the extent of the damage. They told April they believed that both of my legs were broken, and my arm definitely was, but that nothing was certain at this time. Internal damage was a very real worry as well.

When the firemen finally got the truck cut apart with the Jaws of Life and pried the door open, my left leg was in a bind. It had actually been shoved beneath my front seat, if you can even imagine that. I was sitting in the seat, yet my left leg had been completely pushed underneath it. Obviously, that's a problem. I remember one of the firemen saying, "Okay, buddy, we are going to get you out of this truck, but it's going to hurt." I said, "I don't care. Just get me out of this truck." So he and a few other workers grabbed me by my upper body, and they began to pull. They tried to gently remove my leg from under the seat, but it wasn't having it. April says my screams still haunt her today. It was the greatest pain that I had ever felt in my life. Thankfully, a few moments into it, the pain became too great and I passed out. She said after that I was completely silent all the way to the hospital. I don't remember the ride in the ambulance. I only remember waking up beneath bright lights, with dozens of men and women running around me, screaming blood pressures and pulse rates. Doctors yelling out instructions. At this point, I don't recall feeling any pain. But I just recall being scared. All I wanted to do was hold April, Abby, Emma, and Gracee in my arms. Was I going to die?

I was born and raised in church, but I didn't pray near as much as I should. Truth be known, I hadn't been near the Christian I should have been for several years. But at that moment, I prayed. And I prayed hard. I asked God not to take me. *Not now. I know heaven is amazing. I pray that someday I will walk the streets of gold and live in paradise for the rest of eternity, but not today. I want to watch my daughters grow. I want to see them graduate from school and start families of their own. I want to see what they become. I want to spend more time with my beautiful wife. I want her to know she is the best thing that has ever happened to an old bum like me.* I prayed like my life depended on it. And I guess it did. *God, please let me stay a little longer. Please don't take me just yet.*

I remember telling the doctor that we didn't live anywhere near family and my wife needed someone to be with her in the waiting room. So they sent the chaplain out to sit with her. April immediately thought that meant I was going to die, or had already. But he prayed with her and sat with her until some of our friends and family could finally arrive. At this point, everything gets pretty foggy for me. My recollection is not great, but I know I had thousands of prayers go up for me in those days. Friends came and prayed for me, people I'd never met actually had heard about the wreck and came to pray for me, and thousands upon thousands of folks online who loved our family prayed for me. And I believe wholeheartedly that those prayers are why I've been able to write this book. It wasn't my time. God wanted me to be with my children. God wanted me to spend more time with my wife. I had more to add to my story. I wasn't finished.

This year that's coming to a close, 2018, was enormously difficult for me. I had many, many broken bones. I had many, many surgeries and would continue with a few more, a total of twelve once all was said and done, and honestly, I probably have more in my future. I walk with a cane and a very noticeable limp. I can no longer run five miles a day as I did before. I can't build fence or break colts or even ride a horse at all, like I used to. Everyday tasks that were once simple are so difficult, or even impossible. I quickly found myself in a very dark place. I was so depressed, plus plain miserable to be around. I remember looking down at my leg and thinking, *Just raise it, Stoney. Pick your leg up.* But the body wouldn't cooperate. At thirty-eight years old, I was bound to bed for twenty hours a day and was limited to riding a little scooter or being pushed in a wheelchair. I was simply not the man I'd been before.

This year was also enormously difficult on April and our kids. It was difficult on our marriage, because I wasn't exactly easy to live with. April was exhausted for pretty much the entire year as she took care of me and our kids and every aspect of our lives. We struggled. We became somewhat distant with each other, which is a huge change from how we were before. And even though I had miraculously survived a horrible accident, I still hadn't completely given myself and my problems over to God. I was still trying to steer the ship by myself. April sat me down one day and said, "You're still trying to fix everything by yourself, and you can't. Our problem cannot be fixed by you or anyone else. We have to give it to God. *You* have to give it to God. You've just got to trust that God is going to take care of us. He will take care of us. He will keep us safe. But you have to submit. You are our leader. You are our rock. And we need this from you."

At first, I was angry at her for calling me out like that. But after some serious soul-searching, I realized she was right. That message really hit home. For a large part of my adult life, although I certainly considered myself a Christian, I didn't live like one. Before April and the girls, I traveled so much with work, nearly three hundred days a year. So my days were spent in hotels and airports and train stations and rental cars. And my nights were generally spent in a bar somewhere in New York, Massachusetts, North Dakota, Florida, or California, and everywhere in between. I drank myself into oblivion most nights. I was lonely and sad on the inside. This went on for a dozen years, and I am certain I was the focus of many prayers from my parents and siblings. I was unhealthy. I drank too much, didn't eat enough, didn't sleep enough, and was generally unhappy. Then that fateful day when April and I reconnected, everything seemed to change. I felt a joy and a peace I hadn't felt as an adult. Once we were married, I changed jobs and we moved to Texas, and it felt like it was right where God wanted us to be. And even though I knew what I believed, I had never completely given myself to God. Not completely. We went to church, we taught our kids about the Bible, and we raised them to act in a godly manner. But as their dad, I still wasn't living all-in for God. I have read the Bible all the way through four times. I spent hours as a child memorizing Scripture. But knowing isn't enough. You have to use the knowledge.

So that day April called me out, I rededicated myself to God. I prayed and asked forgiveness for all my sins. I apologized for how I have acted for years and for straying away from what I know is right. I believe I am a good person. And I know that I do good deeds and am generous to those in need. But good deeds will not get you into heaven. As Jesus says in John 14:6, "I am the way and the truth and the life. No one comes to the Father except through me." Just being a "good person" doesn't cut it. I began praying more. I began to read my Bible every day. I am a work in progress, but I feel I am on the right track. God has worked in all our lives and brought us closer together. We are stronger and tighter than we have ever been.

I've always heard the saying "Everything happens for a reason." So for most of my life, I've tried to understand the reasons behind something. But the truth is, I kept coming up short. I didn't understand all the bad things in my life. I didn't understand the unhappiness I felt before I found my girls. I didn't understand why God would allow something like that wreck to happen. Why would he allow me to be hurt so bad? Why would he put my wife and kids through such a thing? I no longer believe everything happens for a reason because about all that does is leave you angry at God. I know that was true for me. God never promises us answers to all our questions, but he does promise to be right there with us during our trials and tribulations. And I'm here to tell you, he has been.

Why did I have to go all the way down to the bottom, where I felt I couldn't sink any lower, before I would finally and completely surrender and let God steer my life rather than continuing to aimlessly try to steer it myself? Well, I don't know. Sure, it could have something to do with the fact that I'm a stubborn man. But I'm not sure that's the reason. I'm not angry at God any longer. What I am is grateful. He's never given up on me, although I wouldn't have blamed him if he did. I now prefer the saying "Whatever happens, God's right there with you." I believe that with 100 percent certainty. Actually, make that 110 percent.

⌒⌒⌒⌒⌒

I hope you'll understand,
That I was born a ramblin' man.

Those are the timeless lyrics of the song "Ramblin' Man," written by the amazing Forrest Richard Betts, better known as Dickey Betts of the Allman Brothers Band. If you don't know this song, I'm not sure we can be friends. It's a classic. No, I'm just kidding. I'd still be your friend, but I'd definitely have to work on you and your taste in music.

Since I was just a small boy, I have been a ramblin' man, always with someplace to go, but that meant always leaving too. As a child, I spent countless days and nights on the show circuit, showing everything from horses to cows to pigs. I was on the livestock- and horse-judging teams through my local FFA chapter and traveled extensively all over the United States. My high school had quite the formidable wrestling team, and I was pretty good myself, so I received invitations to wrestle in national tournaments all over the country—in Ohio, Nevada, Texas, and all over Oklahoma. When church camps rolled around every summer, I was ready to go. While my sister would cry because she didn't want to leave home, I was only upset that the camps didn't last longer. I love to travel. I love to see new things and to go to new places. I was never homesick. I always knew that ranch was sitting right there where it had been for more than a hundred years, waiting on me to return.

After I graduated high school, I traveled, and traveled, and kept traveling. I was the ramblin' man with a capital RAMBLE. Following my wreck in November of 2017, it became very clear that we needed to be closer to family. Although our families came down and helped when they could, taking care of my crippled behind was a full-time job. April needed help. She couldn't do it alone. After many discussions and prayers, we decided that moving back to Oklahoma was the answer. Abby had graduated high school and had decided on Oklahoma State University in Stillwater as her next step (which tickled me pink because that's my alma mater too). My parents are in Chickasha, my sister's family is in Yale, my brother's family is in Broken Arrow, and all of April's family is in Vinita. So we worked with my company and got a transfer to Oklahoma. Then began the fun stuff. I'd just had a total hip replacement, then got an infection that required another hip surgery just a week later. April was in an accident with a horse and tore all the ligaments in her right knee except the ACL. Here we are, two people with only two good legs between us, needing to move our entire household of things to Oklahoma. And let me tell you, we had a lot of, well, things. But that's when family comes in awful handy.

My entire family came and moved us, built my fence that was needed for my horses, and did any number of other things we needed for them to do to get us settled into our new house. We are here. Of course, we are still slowly unpacking some of our things, but we are here. Home. We can go eat dinner with my sister with just thirty minutes' notice. We can drop the girls off at their grandparents for a weekend with just a quick phone call. I've never felt more at peace with where I am at in life. My job, the house we are in, my family moving us when we couldn't do it ourselves—everything just fell into place, like puzzle pieces that God had made just for us. I can tell you right now, I don't plan to move again. I am where I want to be. And I think I am where God wants me to be. Sure, to some extent I'll always have that rowdy ramblin' sense about me. That's just who I am. But like Hank Jr. sings, "All my rowdy friends have settled down." That would include me, and I'm more than okay with that. In fact, I'd say I'm downright happy.

P.S. One last story, okay?

He smelled strongly of Aqua Velva. The wind blew the familiar scent my way as I sat on the bench at the Quick-n-Easy Car Wash on Broadway. I've known that smell all my life. I remember as a little boy spending the night with my grandparents, I'd hear my papa wake up early and head to the shower. My granny would start breakfast, and a bit later my papa would come out freshly bathed and shaved, smelling exactly like the smell that currently filled my nostrils. I looked up to see a dapper old man walk up beside me and take a seat. He was small and frail, but that clearly didn't affect the way he dressed. He wore a crisp light blue oxford shirt with the initials JLR stitched into the cuffs, the same polyester Wranglers that my grandpa preferred, and slick, pointy-toed, light orange ostrich Nocona boots. His silver hair was slicked down to his scalp with not a hair out of place. And then, of course, his face was freshly and cleanly shaven.

I expect that at one time he was quite a handsome man. He had a strong jaw, despite his small frame. I remember watching my papa wither away as his Alzheimer's took him away from us. At one time, he was six feet, two inches and weighed 240 pounds. When he died, he was probably five feet, five inches and half of that weight. Judging from this gentleman's big hands, I assumed that this was probably the case for him as well. I was immediately drawn to him. It had been three years since my papa died, and I missed him terribly.

The old man crossed his legs, yet another thing he did that reminded me of my grandfather. "Nice day out, isn't it?" He smiled at me, and I smiled back. "Yes, sir, it's a nice one," I replied. "Supposed to get up to eighty-five degrees today." He seemed to close his eyes and take in as much of the sunshine as possible. I had been drinking a cup of coffee and had finished it. I gently stood up and, with the assistance of my cane, limped over to the trash can about ten feet away. He said, "You're an awful young man to have a limp like that." I laughed and replied, "Yes, sir. About six months ago, I was in a pretty serious car accident. Broke and dislocated my hip, broke my arm, broke a bone in my back, blew out my knee. It was a pretty bad deal." The look of concern on his face was sincere. "My goodness, son. That sounds awful." I showed him a picture of my truck after my accident, sitting in the middle of the road, looking like a crunched Coke can. "Wow. My goodness, my goodness. You're lucky to be alive, I'd say. The good Lord had his hand on you. That's the only way you made it out of that deal alive." I nodded silently, having heard that now for the thousandth time since November 8, 2017.

It can be hard to look at the last six months of my family's life and think about how the Lord has had his hand on us. Since my wreck and injuries, if it could go wrong, it went wrong. The devil can be such a convincing manipulator. He works on us constantly to make us doubt. He prompts questions like *Where was your God when you were having the wreck? Why didn't he save you from that?* I'll be honest, I've asked myself that many times now. But I'm constantly reminded that I could just as easily be dead.

I was brought back to the present when the old man said, "I was working for a logging company in 1957. A chain broke on a truck we'd just loaded, and one of the logs hit me from behind. Broke my back. I had a wife and a one-year-old son at home, and we didn't have any money. I wasn't able to work for six months or so. The church would gather up some money for us every few weeks, and that just barely fed us. We lived in a little two-bedroom house in Henderson, and the landlord was kind to us and let us pay the rent when we could. It was a tough time. Took me a long time to get back to where I could get back out to the logging camp. We ate a lot of beans for a few years." He laughed after he said that last sentence.

I said, "Well, I was lucky, I suppose. I had several fellow employees donate their vacation time to me so that I could continue to get a paycheck. And then when I'd gone through all that, I had some short-term disability benefits that kicked in and paid me until I could get back to work."

He looked at me with an almost-curt look and said, "Not lucky, son. Blessed. I don't like the word *luck*. You've been blessed to have these things. You have a family?" I replied, "Yes, sir. I have three daughters and a wife." He smiled, "That's quite a houseful of women." We both laughed. He said, "I had a wife and a son. My son lives in Atlanta. Some big highfalutin job. Makes a bunch of money. He's divorced, has a daughter and a son. I usually get to see them about once a year. Bert died in 2009." I looked at him and asked, "Bert?" He said, "Roberta. My wife." I nodded my head, silent again. Unsure of exactly what to say. He filled the silence and said, "I've got kidney cancer. Can you believe that?" Surprised, I said, "Oh no . . . really?" He nodded his head. "Yep. Diagnosed me with it last month. Said it's spreading. Gave me about six months to live. Nine if I'm fortunate."

I found myself almost in tears for this man I'd just met. I was having trouble finding the words. He looked at me and grinned. "Now, don't go getting sad on me. That ain't why I told you that. After my accident, it took a while, but I got better and was able to live a long, good life. I'm old now. All my family is gone. My brother died several years ago, and then Bert. I'm not sad, so don't you be either. I get to go see my girl," he said, followed by an almost-childish giggle. Few times in my life have I been rendered utterly speechless, but this was one of those times. Since my accident, I've had such a hard time. But this wonderful little old man at the car wash had just rocked my world with his simple yet powerful words. I looked at him, an old man near the end of his life, sitting in the sunshine with a grin on his face. He has no fear of the end because he knows it's not the end, but the beginning. I never needed that man's message to me more than I needed it that day. The timing could not have been more perfect.

I heard a loud whistle and looked up to see the man who's been cleaning my vehicle, waving a towel above his head letting me know that my truck was finished. I looked over at the old man, and I didn't want to leave. I wanted to sit and talk to him for hours. He stuck his hand out and said, "It was a pleasure talking to you. I hope that limp gets better soon. But I've got faith that it will." I was still struggling to find the words. I grinned at him with tears in my eyes, grabbed his hand, and said, "The pleasure has been all mine, sir. You'll be in my prayers. And I can't wait for you to see Bert." His smile could not have been any bigger. He said, "Me too, son. Me too. What a great day that's going to be." I knew that if I tried to say anything else, I'd probably break down and cry. I nodded at him; he nodded back at me. I turned and headed toward my truck. I tipped the gentleman who had been cleaning my truck, hopped in, and the tears began to flow. I grabbed a tissue out of the console and began to dry my eyes. How lucky I had been to meet this amazing old man, on the very day I needed it so much. No, I reminded myself. Not lucky. *Blessed.*

Acknowledgments

Thank you to my parents, brothers, and sisters for loving me even when I was pretty hard to love and showing me how strong relationships are supposed to be.

Catherine, Marla, and *Do South Magazine,* for giving me my big break and teaching me to be a better writer along the way.

John, thanks for believing in a greenhorn wannabe writer, and thank you for the guidance from start to finish.

My loyal fans, thank you for loving my family and giving us this amazing opportunity.